IMMATURE PEOPLE
WITH
POWER
HOW TO HANDLE THEM

Larry Mullins

2009 Edition

NEW YORK

IMMATURE PEOPLE WITH POWER
HOW TO HANDLE THEM

by LARRY MULLINS

Copyright © 1982 Larry Mullins
Copyright © 2009 Larry Mullins
All rights reserved.

ISBN 978-160037-610-8 (paperback)

Published by:

www.morganjamespublishing.com

Morgan James Publishing, LLC
1225 Franklin Ave. Ste 325
Garden City, NY 11530-1693
Toll Free 800-485-4943
www.MorganJamesPublishing.com

In an effort to support local communities, raise awareness and funds, Morgan James Publishing donates one percent of all book sales for the life of each book to Habitat for Humanity.
Get involved today, visit
www.HelpHabitatForHumanity.org.

TO JOAN

PREFACE
to the New Edition

When it was first published, *Immature People with Power ... How to Handle Them* was a book ahead of its time.

Today people are more willing to believe that there are too many greedy, ruthless and self-serving people running things. Over the years, I have taught the principles of my book to university graduate classes, to nurses, businesspersons, fire-fighters, salespersons, teachers and many others. Basic material from *Immature People with Power* was acquired by the United States Air Force for officer training classes.

Joe Girard, recognized in the *Guinness Book of World Records* for decades as the "World's Greatest Salesperson," has praised *Immature People with Power ... How to Handle Them*: "If I had read Larry Mullins' book when I started out, I would have reached the top much sooner than I did."

This unusual work is the product of a quest to create a self-development program that would be effective in spite of an immature boss, colleague, or other persons who create a negative environment. The methods you will learn in these pages are based upon the tenants of behavioral science. But don't let that scare you. They are simple to master.

The section titled: "The Five Deadly Games that Block the Self-Actualization Process," is unlike anything you may have read before. These principles were distilled from real life experiences and have resonated with seekers of all kinds. Regardless of your personal ambitions, the philosophy of the "five deadly games" will inspire you to take action today and move in the direction of your dreams.

I wrote Immature *People with Power* because I was appalled by the cynical exploitation of employees and managers, and the waste of human potential by too many organizations. I decided to leave corporate perks and go forth on my own, and have never regretted doing so.

A new printing of *Immature People with Power ... How to Handle Them* could hardly be more appropriate and useful, especially in today's business climate. The book is what they call an "easy read." Even so, here you will find timeless, practical ideas and strategies that will quickly elevate your life to new levels of achievement in this era of unprecedented freedom and stimulating challenges.

Larry Mullins

St. Augustine, Florida

CONTENTS

CONTENTS

PART IV — THE FIVE DEADLY GAMES THAT BLOCK THE SELF-ACTUALIZATION PROCESS . . . AND FIVE WAYS TO BANISH THEM FROM YOUR LIFE FOREVER

CONTENTS

A SPECIAL ACKNOWLEDGEMENT TO
HARRY HAIGHT...

without whom this book would never
have been written.

Why This "MANAGEMENT GUIDE" for Employees Was Written

Y OU ARE using about 10% of your potential.

The chances are that you will develop only about 1/10 of your potential even if you live a long and active life.

This is an appalling waste of human resources, and unfortunately typical of the prospects of most human beings.

Yet – if you lived and worked in a nourishing, challenging and supportive environment you could probably achieve splendid things...more things, and better things than you have ever accomplished before.

The odds are very strong that you will never benefit from such an environment – unless *you learn to create it for yourself.*

For over a quarter of a century the entrepreneurs and managers of American businesses have had at their disposal information that could begin to tap the human potential lying fallow in their shops and offices.

This potential could revolutionize the nation.

13

With rare (but important) exceptions, management has failed to study and use this information.

Instead, people who have never read a book on management are too often elevated to important managerial jobs. Often the most ruthless and aggressive employees are rewarded with power and prestige.

These ambitious people are entrusted with the most awesome potential on the planet – human beings.

Because of ignorance and immaturity "managers" squander and destroy this valuable human reservoir of possibilities.

This – in the face of the fact that employee productivity and quality have been proven to be the natural fruits of mature, enlightened and creative management.

Great men like Abraham Maslow, Douglas McGregor, Fredrick Herzberg, and others have studied and analyzed and offered to business a productive new way of cultivating human resources.

Other men, like Robert Townsend, have tried these methods and *proven that they work,* and work with startling effectiveness.

But there are simply not enough mature people to fill the leadership roles in the world.

So Americans, with an opportunity unique in history, still largely work under a psychological tyranny as crippling in its own way as physical brutality was in ages past.

Since management has so much at stake in the status quo, the time has come to offer enlightened management techniques to the employees of America.

It is the workers and "middle managers," with so much to gain, who will be willing to learn a new way of living, who will learn to manage immature authority figures who possess more power than wisdom.

It is employees who will welcome powerful principles that can be applied to unleash their own creative energies.

Here is a helpful guide to developing and actualizing your own vast potentials, even if you must spend a great deal of time in an oppressive, exploitive environment.

This book took many years to write. Each method in it is practical and proven and can usually be immediately applied to real life situations.

This is a simple, easy-to-follow guide, but it will demand the very best you have to offer to apply it and make it work its remarkable results.

Abraham Maslow, the late pioneer of humanistic psychology, liked to ask his college classes this question:

"Who among you will be the great poet, or painter, or entrepreneur, statesman, senator, president or surgeon of your generation?"

This question was always followed by an embarrassed silence, a shuffling of feet and a few giggles.

Then Maslow would ask: "If not you – then *who?*"

My message is this: The world needs more and more idealistic, energetic, compassionate and active people, leaders who trust and believe in the noble potential of the human creature. The world needs people who are willing to expend the energy and make the sacrifices to regain the planet from the weaklings and grown-up "children" who have saturated it with misery and exploitation.

Are you destined to be one of these new leaders?

If not you, then who?

"...old style management is becoming obsolete, putting the enterprise in a less and less advantageous position in competition with other enterprises in the same industry that are under enlightened management and are therefore turning out better products, better service, etc., etc. That is to say that old-style management should soon be obsolete, even in the accounting sense, in the business sense, in the sense of competition, just in the same way that any enterprise will become obsolete and take a bad position in respect to competition if it has obsolete machinery."

ABRAHAM H. MASLOW

Eupsychian Management: A Journal
©1965 by Richard D. Irwin, Inc.
The Dorsey Press   Chicago, Illinois

IMMATURE PEOPLE WITH POWER!

...How to Handle Them

PART I

YES!... YOU <u>CAN</u> FIND FULFILLMENT IN A WORLD THAT BELONGS TO GROWN-UP "CHILDREN"

"WHAT IS THE MEANING OF THIS?" HARRY DEMANDED

H ARRY HAIGHT looked up as the oak door of his office burst open. His heavy jaw dropped as a dozen of his employees marched across his mink rug and menacingly surrounded his desk.

"What is the meaning of this?" Harry demanded.

"The meaning of this is that you are no longer president of this company, Haight," said a usually docile and timid junior executive. Exuding confidence the young man pointed a finger under Harry's nose. "You've bullied and badgered us for the last time. You have exactly five minutes to get off the premises."

Harry rose from his chair. "You're insane!" he shouted. "Get out of here – all of you!"

"Shut up, you old idiot!" snapped Harry's normally mousey

secretary. Then she reached into her purse and pulled out a pistol! As she leveled it at Harry's ample stomach she snarled: "We aren't kidding fatso! You have four minutes left!"

Sweat began to bead on Harry's face as he snatched the phone from the desk. "Quick," he ordered the operator, "get me the police."

'Oh, go to hell!" shouted the operator, and then the phone went dead with a loud click.

"Three minutes," said Mrs. Perkins as her hand tightened ominously on the pistol.

It was a terrified Harry Haight who scurried from the building he had ruled with an iron hand for 14 years. His company limousine had disappeared from his private parking place, along with the sign that had designated the spot as his. So Harry made his way along the freeway on foot, his arms loaded with as many office mementos as he could carry.

Harry Haight was found a few days later, babbling incoherent orders to trees and stones.

He never recovered his sanity . .

HARRY HAIGHT WAS FOUND A FEW DAYS LATER . . .

1

You Live
In A World Of
DANGEROUS "CHILDREN"

...The First Essential to Gaining
Freedom is Finding Out Why

WOULDN'T it be nice if we could get rid of the emotionally incompetent bosses in the world by throwing them out! If only the Harry Haights of this world could be deposed like some tyrannical South American dictator!

But alas, this cannot be. We are stuck, for the time being, with these "children."

So the Harry Haights of this world go on destroying employee's careers, ruining marriages, and squandering human resources and potentials.

Unfortunately, at this stage of evolution, the world belongs to emotional "children" like Harry Haight. Virtually every major problem facing civilization today stems from the fact that there are not enough mature people available to assume the leadership roles of the planet.

Not only must we deal with immature bosses, but also immature and obnoxious policemen, mechanics, lawyers, salespeople, clergymen, politicians, doctors, petty clerks, and so on.

23

Many aggressive and ruthless people get positions of authority and power. They often have the means to disturb the flow of our own lives.

Society is burdened with too many people who have powers of *execution* beyond their powers of *understanding*. Unfortunately, while these individuals have the power to disturb the well-being of others, they have not developed the sensitivity and wisdom to use this power with restraint and compassion.

The grown up "children" who run this world are not bad or evil people. It is simply that they have immature values and seek to satisfy immature needs.

THE HOPE OF MANKIND: EXCEPTIONAL PEOPLE.

On the other hand we cannot deny that now and then a rare exception stands out against this foil of human mediocrity.

The world has been blessed, on rare occasions, with a special human being such as a Lincoln, or a Helen Keller, or a Toscanini.

These exceptional, unique human beings are not motivated, carrot and stick, the way the rest of us are. Their values transcend the ordinary (such values are called "meta values").

They live as though they have some special pipeline to power and knowledge that is not possessed by the rest of us.

These exceptional people are the hope of mankind. They exemplify, not so much what mankind is, but rather what *it could be*. When one of these relatively mature people gravitate to a position of power, beautiful things begin to happen.

In business the person who acquires power is, of course, called the boss. More and more it is being recognized that a boss is most effective when he is a mature person.

For example, now and then, a man like Robert Townsend comes along. He was responsible for the Avis success in the mid-sixties. When this idealistic man took Avis over, things looked bleak. For the thirteen previous years Avis had failed to make a tangible profit.

THEORY "Y" AND THEORY "X"

As the new president of Avis, Townsend applied the humanistic management principles of Abraham Maslow and Douglas McGregor. Townsend admits he applied these enlightened methods rather crudely, sort of feeling his way along. He credits these new methods, called "Theory Y," with the dramatic turnaround of the Avis Company.

"Theory Y" management is human, sensitive, aggressive management. It is based upon the premise that under *natural* and *nourishing* circumstances, workers will assume responsibility, and they will be generally creative and independent in their approach to problems.

Theory Y has an underlying faith that human beings are basically good and self-motivated under natural and nourishing circumstances. (This is an important distinction.)

Not many businessmen apply Theory Y principles. I have heard many ruthless and acquisitive entrepreneurs pay lip service to high-sounding management theories. But when the chips are down, and the pressure is on, they always fall back on their real principles, those of *Theory X*.

Theory X holds that employees are lazy, shiftless, and untrustworthy; and management must drive and coerce them. Fear is the master weapon of such management. It works most effectively if employees are made to feel insecure.

Military organizations are traditionally run by the Theory X (fear) methods. This theory works effectively when the boss is able to threaten and actually carry out his threats.

In the business world, the fear methods of Theory X worked better years ago than they do today. People are more sophisticated today, and they are harder to intimidate.

If a worker is not protected by some union and if he is fired, he has various government assistance programs he can fall back upon. In this country, at this time, few people really face starvation if they lose their job.

So fear has become less and less effective as a management "tool." In order to motivate today's employees, it is necessary to understand and cultivate higher human needs. Safety, or fear of losing one's security, is vastly diminished as a need factor in the world of today.

Theory Y is an attempt to appeal to the higher human motivations. Theory Y is a flexible concept, and takes into consideration the fact that workers have tremendous drives to fulfill their unsatisfied wants and desires.

For example, a shrewd management often promotes a very active union man into an executive position. Management knows that an ambitious person has powerful drives for independence, for ego food and control.

When an energetic union leader is placed into management responsibilities, he must, of course, give up his union activities. He soon discovers that the satisfaction of his ego needs is now dependent on the company, not the union members.

Soon the former union man begins to expedite company policy with great vigor. Some of the toughest company managers, and harshest Theory X bosses, were once union champions for the rights of workers.

Theory Y is also known as "humanistic management." It is a good theory, but it is more difficult than Theory X to administer. To be adroit at using Theory Y a manager must be mature, strong, and wise.

Does Theory Y work? Well, let's see what happened when Robert Townsend used it.

When Robert Townsend took over the Avis company he began to apply Theory Y. He found that it was more risky and adventurous than Theory X. And soon he began to get favorable results.

THE AVIS MIRACLE

Under Theory Y management, Avis sales jumped from 30 million in sales to 75 million. Profit, during this three year climb were respectable: one million, then three million, and finally five million.

In his fascinating book <u>UP THE ORGANIZATION</u>, Townsend explains that he achieved the Avis "miracle" without wholesale hiring and firing. He took over a management staff that was demoralized and labeled "losers." He began to redirect and inspire their talents.

Three years after taking over this "hopeless" management staff, Townsend was visited by the President of ITT, Hal Greenen. Mr. Greenen was impressed by the "new" Avis, especially the management.

"I have never seen such depth in management," Greenen said. Yet, Townsend confesses that this was virtually the same management team that was once considered "hopeless."

SO, WHY ISN'T THEORY Y USED BY EVERY BUSINESS?

Good question.

If good management is so profitable, one would imagine that profit-hungry companies would go to any lengths to apply it.

The answer may be quite simple.

When Townsend took over Avis as president, he had the authority to make sweeping changes. He believed in, and was dedicated to, the humanistic values of Theory Y management.

If Townsend had not possessed the ultimate authority to use Theory Y principles, and the resolution to keep using them, he would have failed.

UNLESS THE TOP BOSS BELIEVES IN AND UNDERSTANDS SOUND MANAGEMENT PRINCIPLES, NO MANAGER UNDER HIM CAN CONSISTENTLY APPLY THEM AND MAKE THEM WORK.

No matter how well-intentioned, an immature top executive cannot run a company on mature principles. As soon as the first crisis hits, it's back to old-fashioned threats and fear tactics.

When an idealistic, new manager graduates from college, the immaturity of the real world hits him with stunning impact. Such a person was never trained to cope with an immature power stucture.

Generally, aspiring managers and executives are taught logical theory and sensible application of that theory. What they actually see in practice is an entirely different thing.

Very few, if any, businesses are "run by the book." Most often businesses operate on about the same "emotional" level as the chief executive. Many businesses are actually hostile to mature management concepts.

Imagine! The most precious, under-rated, and potentially powerful forces on the planet – human resources – are often under the stewardship of clumsy, immature, and insensitive individuals!

YOU CAN BECOME A GUERRILLA INFILTRATOR

Robert Townsend was in an ideal position to make broad changes in company policy. He recognized, however, that most of us won't be so fortunate. So he suggested an alternative solution.

Townsend suggested that there are two general attitudes we can adopt toward our jobs. We can sell out to the company, grab all the benefits and money we can, and say the hell with the rest of humanity. Or, we can fight the immaturity of a monster-type company with non-violent guerrilla warfare.

This book is a manual for conducting nonviolent guerrilla warfare in an immature company.

This book will teach you how to manage your immature boss, and other people with more power than they know how to handle.

Managing an immature person is not easy, especially when the person happens to be your boss.

But – learning to manage immature people is very, very rewarding.

Before you can manage anything, however, you must first learn the Master Key. Ernest Hemingway called this key: "Grace Under Pressure."

Let's see what this Master Key is, and how it works.

POINTS TO REMEMBER:

—SOCIETY IS BURDENED by too many people who have powers of EXECUTION beyond their powers of UNDERSTANDING ... we live in a world of grown-up, powerful "children."

—THEORY X is management by FEAR and INTIMIDATION.

—THEORY Y is management by the cultivation of higher human potentials.

THIS BOOK is a manual for the conducting of non-violent guerrilla warfare ... for the purpose of making a monster company a bit more human.

REFERENCES:

Robert Townsend: <u>UP THE ORGANIZATION</u>, Alfred F. Knopf, New York, 1976

Douglas McGregor: <u>THE HUMAN SIDE OF ENTERPRISE</u>, McGraw-Hill Book Company, New York, 1960

Dale Carnegie: <u>HOW TO WIN FRIENDS AND INFLUENCE PEOPLE</u>, Simon and Schuster, Inc. (Pocket Books), New York, 102nd printing, 1975

Abraham Maslow: <u>EUPSYCHIAN MANAGEMENT</u>, Richard D. Irwin, Inc., and The Dorsey Press, 1965

H.A. Overstreet: <u>THE MATURE MIND</u>, W.W. Norton & Company, New York, 1949

A HORRIFIED HUSH CAME OVER THE CROWD OF DELEGATES

IT WAS a grey, somber winter day in Moscow. Nikita Khrushchev had been speaking at the meeting of Soviet delegates for some time.

Khrushchev explained in some detail why he maintained strong government control over the arts in Russia. He took special efforts to point out that a greater degree of freedom was enjoyed by artists under his regime, compared to the tyranny of Joseph Stalin.

A delegate rose and took exception to the cosmetic changes Khrushchev had made. The delegate asserted that there was still an atmosphere of oppression. He was a writer and he complained of the tight restraints that burdened him.

Nikita Khrushchev's face became scarlet. The veins in his neck swelled; his eyes bulged. He leaned forward menacingly, and his lips began to tremble. He pointed a powerful finger at the Russian writer before him.

"There was a time," Khrushchev roared, "when a remark like that would get you a bullet in the head!"

A horrified hush came over the crowd of delegates. They knew the courageous writer had spoken up to the wrong man. Now the Premier was in one of his violent and dangerous states of mind.

The writer raised his head and stared directly at Khrushchev. "I had imagined that we had progressed beyond such a time," he said coldly.

The audience broke into spontaneous applause. Khrushchev nodded agreement. He had been stopped. He could not retaliate. There would be no repercussions. The brave Russian writer had triumphed ... he had used the master key: grace under pressure.

2

The Master
Key to Winning:
GRACE UNDER PRESSURE

**. . . . If You Can't Learn This,
You're in for a Life of Torment**

IMAGINE the cool of that Russian artist . . . facing a temper tantrum of one of the most powerful men on earth without even blinking!

And herein lies a key secret of all achievement: KEEP YOUR COOL.

If you cannot control yourself, your immature boss will control you.

Even if you must get angry, to be effective you must have your anger under control and possess a clear, poised mind.

There is no other way.

Do you recall some of the many times you lost your temper, and then regretted it? Remember the insensitive, stupid waiters, the sullen parking attendants, the nasty sales clerks? Remember how they got to you?

Did you gain anything by losing your temper? *Never! You have gained nothing, and you have paid and paid and paid.* At least you gained nothing by an immature tantrum that could not have been achieved more gracefully by *righteous anger under mature control.*

The tough gang members in the slums know this. The great athletes know this. The great statesmen know this. John Kennedy often quoted Hemingway's phrase for it: "Grace under pressure."

Any good actor uses this secret. Anger is most effective when it is held in restraint...when it seems to be a shadow of a deeper, powerful fire raging within. As the great Enrico Caruso observed: "The secret of art is restraint." When Caruso sang there always seemed to be a deep reservoir of untapped power behind the voice of gold.

There can be no question: there will be times when you must take a firm and fearless position with your immature boss. There may come a time when the only thing you can do is resign. *But, do so at your own convenience, never, never in a fit of temper.*

You must be so dedicated to your own long range self-interest that you can avoid the immediate self-indulgence of a temper-tantrum.

WHY DOES THE BOSS LOSE HIS TEMPER?

Did Khrushchev really lose control of his temper? What was he trying to do, intimidate the poor man who dared question his policies?

Why does a boss lose his temper?

A BOSS LOSES HIS TEMPER TO GET HIS OWN WAY.

Khrushchev was communicating with his words and body language: "I am angry and dangerous because you have said (or done) something I don't like. If you do not back down and stop doing (or saying) this, I will become angrier. If you wish me to stop being angry, you must behave in a way that is acceptable to me."

When a boss becomes angry and shouts abuse at a timid employee, the boss usually succeeds in intimidating him. This is a Theory X method. The boss may use other techniques, such as becoming sullen, scowling, being uncommunicative and withdrawn. In each case he is exhibiting "get my way" behavior.

Most bosses with "bad tempers" simply have become conditioned to getting their way by blowing up. It works with timid employees and managers, so they continue to do it.

This is why people too often vent their anger at their children. Children are easy to frighten. They can be kept "in line" with fear. One day the child grows up, and is no longer so afraid. That is when the Theory X parent loses control.

Doesn't it seem ridiculous that a boss is able to get his way by "losing his temper" and intimidating grown men and women?

It is not logical that such immature *"get my way"* tactics are employed. It is equally illogical that such tactics should succeed with so many people. *But immature people are not logical.*

This is the second critical point: Do not waste logical arguments on an immature boss.

A furniture salesman taught me this valuable lesson about fifteen years ago: Believe it or not, *about 95% of the people you meet will not be persuaded or motivated by purely logical arguments.*

THE SURPRISING SECRET OF A MASTER SALESMAN

Many years ago I was giving a sales training meeting to a group of furniture salesmen in a Washington, D.C. store. I carefully prepared my talk, and believed it was a great contribution to the art of selling.

To me, back then, selling was logical. I read all the books. It was a simple matter of convincing people that a particular item is worth more than the money asked for it.

Imagine for a moment that you are a professional salesperson. If you wish to convince a prospect of the worth of the thing you are selling, you must first point out all the benefits they

will enjoy by owning the item. You have to support these benefits with specific product points or features that make the
benefits possible.

For example, you do not *sell* a mattress, you sell refreshing
sleep, better health, more energy. You support these potential
benefits (and make them believable) by pointing out the generous padding on the mattress, the resilient steel springs, and
so on. These product features make your claim of better sleep
plausible. If you do your job well, you can create, in the
customer's mind, an abstract vision of a better life, a brand
new happier self.

It is all very logical.

If you fail to get your customer to part with his money, you
have simply failed to convince him of enough benefits. As soon
as the benefits outweigh the value of the money asked, a sale
will be made.

This is old stuff to any salesperson. In the sales training
meeting I prepared I tried to give some fresh insights into this
classic, and very logical sales sequence. As I spoke on the day
of the meeting, I noticed that one of the best veteran salesmen
was not paying much attention.

After I finished my talk I approached the bored salesman,
who was named Ted Grady. I was a bit annoyed at his indifferent attitude to my presentation, but I tried to conceal this. I
asked Ted to join me for a cup of coffee.

"Ted," I said over the cafeteria table, "you have been in this
business a long time. You are a natural at selling. Just as Mickey
Mantle doesn't need lessons in the fundamentals of batting, you
don't need them in the fundamentals of selling. But most of
the other salesmen do. I thought maybe you could tell me how to
make my talk more interesting to the accomplished pros
like yourself."

Ted looked at me with a twinkle in his bright blue eyes.
I think he saw through my attempt at diplomacy.

"Do you know what is wrong with your ideas?" Ted asked.
"They are too logical."

"What!" I was incredulous. "All selling is based upon logic.
It has to be!"

"That's fine for theories, *but people aren't logical!*" Ted stopped a moment to sip his coffee. "See, theory does not interest me because I have to make my living out on the sales floor. If I don't sell, I don't eat!

"I would imagine," Ted went on, "that about 95% of the people I talk to are not logical. They are emotional. Oh, now and then I get a mature customer who is primarily interested in the product features and benefits of a piece of furniture. With these people I can use the logical, classic sales methods.

"The other people, the 95%, don't seem to care as much about the construction of a bedroom suite or the quality of a cushion on a sofa. At least, that is not the most important thing to these people."

I was astonished. "If the features and quality of an item are not the most important thing to these people, what is?"

"That all depends," Ted said. That made me smile, and Ted noted it. "No, I'm not copping out when I say 'it depends!' It really does. It depends upon what type of person I am talking to."

Ted was getting excited as he went on. "You see, Larry, some people come in to shop for furniture with a chip on their shoulder. They are primarily interested in showing me who's boss. They pick an argument over some trifle, and they make obnoxious, unfair statements. Other folks will barely talk at all. They don't seem to trust anyone, and they are very difficult to communicate with. Other people yak and yak and show me pictures of their kids, and generally try to make friends with me. I guess they think they'll get a better deal this way.

"Now, if I try to be logical with the obnoxious, aggressive type of person, he will just argue with everything I say. If I try pure logic on the withdrawn person, he will not believe me and will pull further away. And the overly friendly individual would be bored by a logical sales presentation.

"So my job is to find ways to make each of these types respond to my sales presentation. I have to find the psychological 'buttons' of each of these people. I have to know when to 'push' these 'buttons,' and how.

"And that is a lot of trouble, but it is well worth it. Customers are my bosses. They pay my salary. I must learn to work with each of them, in spite of their immaturities."

Ted and I became good friends after this conversation. He was indeed a master salesman, and I began to watch him more closely. I noted, most of all, how Ted was flexible in his relationships. He could be as tough as the toughest customer and as pleasant as the nicest.

He always seemed to be in control of the situation. He seemed to be able to untrack an immature customer's "game plan" and steer the conversation into those channels that would assure a sale.

YOU ARE A SALESPERSON

Here is the critical point: *A salesman's relationship with his customers closely parallels your relationship with your boss.*

In a way, if you are an ambitious person, you are trying to "sell" your boss on your own abilities and talents.

Around the turn of the century Charles M. Schwab was a brilliant employee of Andrew Carnegie. He was also a great salesman. Schwab sold J. P. Morgan the idea of buying the Carnegie steel interests. Schwab then became the President of the resulting trust: United States Steel. Not bad for a young man of 35!

Schwab once said, "We are all salespeople, every day of our lives. We are selling our ideas, our plans, our energies and our enthusiasms to those with whom we come in contact."

Nearly all really great individuals were master "salespeople." For example: Lincoln, Churchill, Eleanor Roosevelt were masters at selling. (Some masters at selling were immature, unscrupulous con men, like Hitler!) But every human being who has had *impact on the world* for good or evil, was exceptional at selling his ideas and projecting his personality.

The great people, the mature people of this world, are exceedingly careful in their day-to-day human relationships.

As a matter of fact, one critical difference between you and any great person may well be this single factor: *Great people take precautions in their ordinary human relationships that lesser people fail to bother with.*

When Teddy Roosevelt returned to the White House for a brief visit, the servants and gardeners swarmed around him. Some were weeping in joy just to see him again. They reacted this way because Roosevelt treated them with respect and compassion.

There is a scene in the play *Our Town* in which a young teenage girl pleads with her mother to look at her just once "as though you really *see* me."

HOW TO DOUBLE YOUR "CHARISMA"

Actors and politicians have a trick that makes them seem dynamic even when they are simply listening to someone else. They concentrate very hard on *how* the other person is saying what he is saying.

David Niven, the actor, learned this the hard way. When his first movie was played for a small group of Hollywood elite back in 1935, Niven pressed Charlie Chaplin for an opinion of his role. Finally Chaplin said: "You act well, but you listen poorly. You must learn to *listen* to the other actors."

You can be just as effective in a conversation when you actively *listen* to and *really see* the other person, as when you are actually speaking. In fact, you will quickly double your charisma by simply paying attention to the other person.

The technique of active listening applies equally in your relationship with your boss. *Really* see him, and *really* listen to him.

You will see an immediate change, especially if you practice remaining cool, and objective, and poised at the same time.

Of course, handling ill-tempered people is very difficult, and we will treat the subject in detail later. For the time being, simply practice active listening and composure.

THE ONE THING YOU CAN CONTROL

You can always maintain control of your half of a relationship. But that is all. It is up to the other guy to control his half.

Your success in handling other people will always be predicated upon your ability to control your own responses. No matter how immature your boss may act, *you can always respond in a mature manner.*

The techniques in this book are based upon practical experience, and the work of Abraham Maslow, and a host of other psychologists. (Don't worry, we will not offer you a lot of theories or formulas to study.)

I have seen salesmen with average IQ's quickly master the techniques we will disclose. I have also seen these methods work wonders on a relationship with an immature boss.

These methods are broadly called COMPASSIONATE/ASSERTION.

Compassionate/Assertion is based upon discoveries in behavioral science that are astonishingly effective, yet easy to master.

People completely new to the system pick it up in an hour or so, and if they have good horse sense, they can begin to put it to immediate use.

Is your mind open? Good! Get ready for some revolutionary ideas!

POINTS TO REMEMBER:

— IF YOU CANNOT control yourself, you cannot control situations: KEEP YOUR COOL, THE BOSS LOSES HIS TEMPER TO GET HIS WAY.

A MOST FASCINATING CASE OF "GET MY WAY" BEHAVIOR . . .

— YOU CAN ONLY CONTROL one half of any relationship, your own half.

START HANDLING YOUR HALF OF RELATIONSHIPS MATURELY, AND FORGET ABOUT THE OTHER HALF.

I UNDERSTAND . . .

— THE DIFFERENCE between success and mediocrity is often the degree of care in which a person treats his relationships. REALLY SEE PEOPLE, HEAR PEOPLE, AND BE AWARE OF WHAT YOU SAY TO THEM.

41

REFERENCES:

Ewing T. Webb and John B. Morgan, Ph.D.: STRATEGY IN HANDLING PEOPLE, Garden City Publishing Company, New York, 1930

Abraham Maslow: THE FARTHER REACHES OF HUMAN NATURE, Viking Press, New York, 1973

Elmer Wheeler: HOW TO SELL YOURSELF TO OTHERS, Prentice-Hall Inc., New York, 1947

James T. Mangan: THE KNACK OF SELLING YOURSELF, Pocket Books, New York, 1968

John Narcisco and David Burkett: DECLARE YOURSELF — DISCOVERING THE ME IN RELATIONSHIPS, Prentice-Hall Inc., Englewood Cliffs, New Jersey, 1975

Ernest Dichter: MOTIVATING HUMAN BEHAVIOR, McGraw-Hill, New York, 1971

Neil and Margaret Rau: ACT YOUR WAY TO SUCCESSFUL LIVING, Wilshire Book Company, Hollywood, California, 1968

PART II:

THE MYSTERY OF BEHAVIOR MADE SIMPLE
(The "Secret" Forces That Pull Your Boss' Strings) . . .

AND MOTIVATION THE EASY WAY
(How to Stop Pushing and Begin Being Pulled)

"UH-OH . . . A RED-82!"

I magine this situation: You are driving down the highway on a pleasant Sunday afternoon. In the rearview mirror you suddenly notice a car moving up fast on the road behind you.

Although you are going just over the speed limit, this car goes quickly by you on the right lane.

As the car goes by, you observe a red sign above the license plate with numerals "82" on it. You murmur to yourself: "Uh-oh . . . a RED 82!" and immediately you ease up on the throttle and become very cautious.

Without warning or a signal, the car suddenly cuts in front of you and zooms on at very high speed. Relaxed again, you settle back and continue to enjoy your ride.

This imaginary story is based upon an impractical (but intriguing) theory of mine: If drivers were required to post their IQ scores on their cars, it would eliminate many accidents.

Obviously, if you spotted an "82" IQ sign on a car, you would anticipate the possibility of the driver making a less than intelligent move.

In addition, if the driver in question did do something dangerous and stupid, you'd be much more likely to take it philosophically. After all, what can you expect from an 82 IQ?

But – you might ask – what about the immature driver, the one with a high IQ who is still emotionally a child?

We'd simply give mature people GREEN signs, and those of emotional incompetence RED SIGNS! So, if you should see a car with a RED "149" on it, you'd exercise keen caution.

Of course, as I said, the idea is not practical, and neither is the one that follows:

Imagine if immature, ruthless and aggressive people were required to wear RED armbands! Be simple to spot them then, wouldn't it?

THE FACT IS: IMMATURE PEOPLE DO GIVE OFF UNMISTAKABLE SIGNALS THAT CLEARLY REVEAL THEIR NATURES AND THEIR SECRET INNER NEEDS!

It is true that no two people are alike. It is equally true, however, that people tend to act in patterns. We acknowledge this when we say something like: "Jane is a sweet, considerate person," or "Jim just isn't himself today!"

Important developments in Behavioral Science have given us the keys to "read" the signals of other people and actually predict, in a general way, their behavior.

Let's learn the system now, and put it to the acid test tomorrow. I promise you, you will never look at people in quite the same way again!

3

How To
READ YOUR
BOSS LIKE A BOOK

**...Recognize, in a Flash, those Clues Your Boss Cannot
Hide... and Learn What these Signals Reveal
about His Secret Inner Needs**

B EFORE you can READ your boss it is necessary to RATE him.
The rating system we shall use has two scales: HOSTILITY/
COMPASSION and ASSERTIVENESS/TIMIDNESS.

You might ask: "How can we measure such intangibles? How
compassionate is compassionate? And how hostile is hostile?"

Behavioral Scientists tell us that there are no absolutes in
human behavior... that there is really no ultimate degree of
hostility or compassion.

However, like musical scales, which theoretically can go on
forever in each direction (higher or lower), hostility and compassion can be measured in relative terms.

To illustrate this, let's imagine a completely indifferent individual, no hostility and no compassion. (Impossible for a normal person, but imagine it anyway.) Let's place this individual at ground zero, in the theoretical center of the hostility/compassion scale.

Now imagine the scale going off in either direction, one side toward hostility, and the other toward compassion:

You recall that we said that there are no absolutes in human behavior, or final "stopping places" at either end of the scale. But for the sake of clarity, let's establish arbitrary designations of 1 to 10 on each side of the scale. (We agree, even when we do this, that no human being could reach the absolute degree of "10" on either side of the scale.)

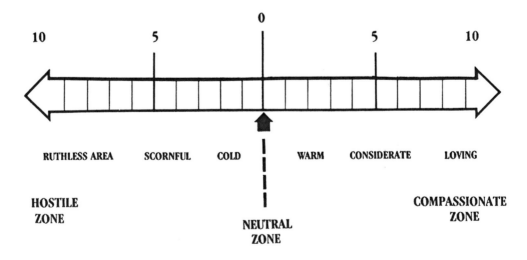

Now decide which *side* of the scale your boss should be rated. This should not be difficult.

To help you determine upon which side your boss belongs, imagine which descriptive words would be most appropriate to describe him.

Words that best describe a compassionate nature are warmth, trust, sensitivity, sincerity, kindness, openness, sympathy, helpfulness, consideration, tact, graciousness, and benevolence. Would these apply to your boss?

If these words don't fit his behavior, perhaps he should be placed on the hostile side of the scale. In this case, he would be more appropriately described by words like scornful, indifferent, arrogant, insensitive, brutal, cold, aloof, and ruthless.

The actual degree of hostility or warmth with which you "credit" your boss is less significant than the *side of the scale upon which you place him.* This should not be difficult for you to decide.

For purposes of illustration, let's suppose you have a boss like Harry Haight. Of course, he would be placed on the hostile side of the scale, ranging almost to ruthless.

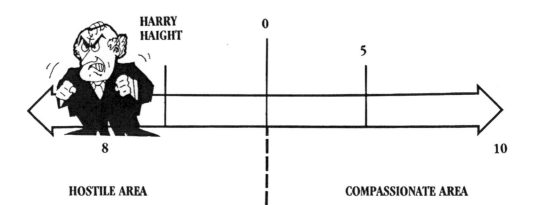

While you keep in mind where you have placed your own boss on the HOSTILITY/COMPASSION scale, let's go on to the second part of our system and rate your boss on ASSERTIVENESS/TIMIDNESS.

RATING YOUR BOSS ON HIS DRIVE

How would you score your boss' courage, drive and ambition?

As we did with compassion, we need to establish an imaginary scale with a neutral point in the middle. In this neutral point we place a completely passive individual; he neither retreats timidly nor advances aggressively in his life situations.

Now, let's place extremely aggressive behavior at the top of the scale, and acutely timid behavior at the bottom.

For the sake of clarity, we will again establish our arbitrary designations of 1-10 at each end of the scale.

Using the same approach as before, where would you rate your boss on this scale?

Descriptive words for the aggressive top part of the scale would be: leadership, confidence, authoritative manner, initiative, a drive to control, ambition, and so on.

Aggressive people like to get in the mainstream of life and affect things. They desire to have impact on the world, to put their stamp on the world, to establish evidence that "they've been here."

On the opposite pole of our scale is timidness. Timidness is more than simple passiveness; it is a fearful retreat from life.

A timid person has the tendency to avoid the limelight, to shrink from responsibility, to be compliant, (or at least pretend to be compliant!) and to be self-defeating.

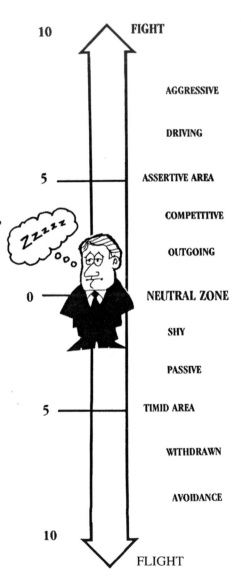

- 10   FIGHT
- AGGRESSIVE
- DRIVING
- 5   ASSERTIVE AREA
- COMPETITIVE
- OUTGOING
- 0   NEUTRAL ZONE
- SHY
- PASSIVE
- 5   TIMID AREA
- WITHDRAWN
- AVOIDANCE
- 10   FLIGHT

Timid people believe safety and security are more important than the risk of proving their own value or worth. There is a propensity to strive to maintain the status quo of situations. Passive people believe that facing a known evil is better than facing the unknown, because they fear it might be even worse!

Of course we know that Harry Haight is certainly not passive or timid. He is driving and ambitious. Using Harry again as an example, we would place him on an 8 or so on the aggressive side of the scale.

Now we have two fixes on Harry. He is extremely hostile and extremely aggressive.

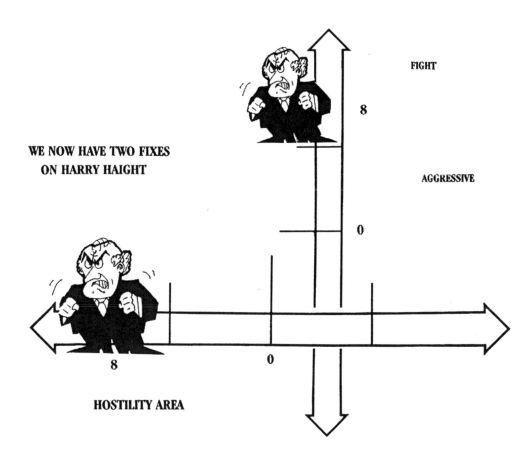

We are now ready to put Harry "together." When we combine the two characteristics of Ruthlessness and Aggressiveness, here is what we come up with as a profile, or "model" of Harry Haight:

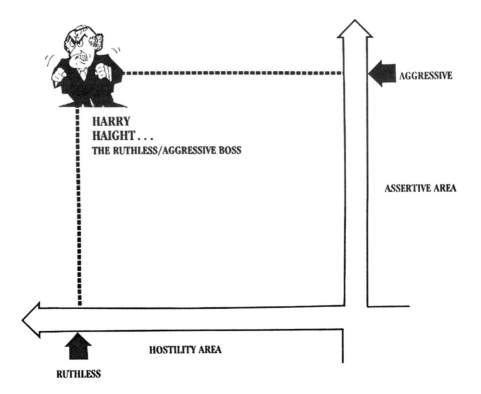

HARRY
HAIGHT...
THE RUTHLESS/AGGRESSIVE BOSS

AGGRESSIVE

ASSERTIVE AREA

HOSTILITY AREA

RUTHLESS

PUTTING YOUR OWN BOSS TOGETHER

You have now rated your *own* boss on each scale: HOSTILITY/ COMPASSION and ASSERTIVENESS/TIMIDNESS. You are ready for the next step, putting him together.

You recall that we rated Harry as an "8" RUTHLESS and as an "8" AGGRESSIVE. If we extend lines from each scale until they meet (as in the diagram) we get an idea how extreme a Ruthless/Aggressive boss can be! Extend your own boss' ratings in this manner and you will discover that he falls into one of four distinct categories:

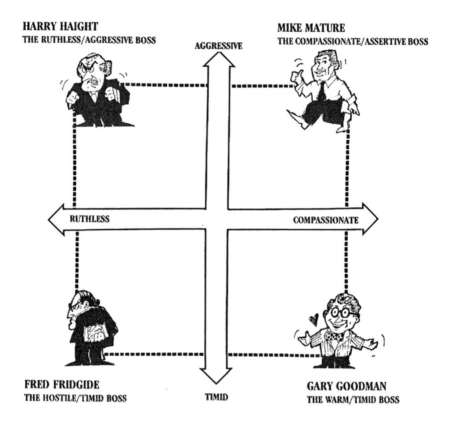

HARRY HAIGHT
THE RUTHLESS/AGGRESSIVE BOSS

MIKE MATURE
THE COMPASSIONATE/ASSERTIVE BOSS

AGGRESSIVE

RUTHLESS

COMPASSIONATE

FRED FRIDGIDE
THE HOSTILE/TIMID BOSS

TIMID

GARY GOODMAN
THE WARM/TIMID BOSS

If you rated your boss as both aggressive and hostile, he is a RUTHLESS/AGGRESSIVE type, similar to Harry Haight.

If your boss is hostile, but on the withdrawn side, you have a HOSTILE/TIMID boss, a man we call FRED FRIDGIDE.

If your boss is compassionate and sensitive, yet at the same time is passive and timid, you have a GARY GOODMAN boss, or a WARM/TIMID boss.

The final possibility is that you have a relatively mature boss, who is driving and assertive but also manifests a healthy concern about others and respects their feelings. In this case he is a COMPASSIONATE/ASSERTIVE boss, and we'll call him MIKE MATURE.

For the rest of this book we will refer to these four types of bosses. These are extreme "models," and such extreme types rarely exist in real life.

If a psychologist wrote a personality profile on your boss, it would probably be complex and difficult to understand. And, after you read it, it would be hard for you to apply the knowledge you gained. There would simply be too much data to be of much value.

For this reason we are using the model approach in dealing with your boss. The essentials of a boss' behavior can be boiled down and conceptionalized in a character like Harry Haight. Even though these examples are imaginary models of extremes in behavior types, they are very valuable as reference points from which to judge your own boss.

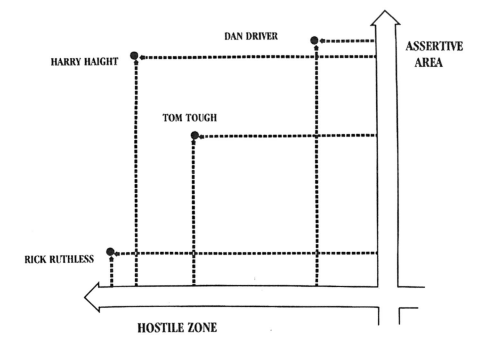

NOBODY ACTS EXACTLY AS SOMEONE ELSE WOULD

Keep in mind also that within each of the four areas there exists an infinite number of variations. Your own boss may be very ruthless, but only moderately aggressive. Or the other way around, he could be only moderately hostile yet extremely aggressive.

Any of the bosses shown in the diagram may be accurately designated as R/A types, or RUTHLESS/AGGRESSIVE. Yet, as you can see, each is entirely unique in personality and temperament.

THE LIMITATIONS TO "TYPECASTING"

– Human beings can never be comfortably pigeon-holed. Each person will show flashes of uncharacteristic behavior at times. We acknowledge this when we say so-and-so "isn't being himself today."
– People vary in their roles. Harry Haight may be the most ruthless and aggressive of bosses, and yet may be a docile Gary Goodman around his wife. He may, on the other hand, be utterly ruthless with men employees and wishy-washy with women employees.
– People can put up a front. This is called a "mask tactic," and is used to disguise the real attitudes of the person using it.
We will learn how to detect and expose these behaviors.
– Under extreme stress, people can act differently. This is called a "frustration behavior." Push a Gary Goodman too far, and even he can act like Harry Haight, for a short period.

TIME TO PAUSE: WHAT TYPE ARE YOU?

If you are like most people, you grasped the idea about personality types quickly. You may surprise yourself as you are quickly able to determine the general personality type of your boss, your spouse, and your friends.

It is also important to know what type of personality you possess. This is because your boss' behavior is greatly affected by your own.

For example, Harry Haight acts differently with another aggressive person than he does with a timid type of person. So the attitude that *you* project will cause him to act differently.

If you are an employee of the Compassionate/Assertive type, you have a tremendous advantage in dealing with your immature boss. The reason for this is your own needs will not conflict with his; you will not be fighting for the same "ego food," so to speak.

So, how do you develop into a Compassionate/Assertive type of person? How do you become more assertive and yet retain your warmth and compassion for others?

We know that your behavior and attitudes do not just "happen." Your own personality type is based upon your beliefs about YOURSELF and OTHER PEOPLE.

The more POSITIVE these beliefs are, the better off you are.

How would you rate yourself, using the same methods you rated Harry Haight? To help a little, check out the EMPLOYEE BELIEFS page, and honestly see which comes closest to your own.

We know we cannot change Harry Haight, so a key objective of this book is to help you begin to develop the poise and assertiveness you need to deal with Harry Haight, Fred Fridgide, Gary Goodman and yes, even Mike Mature.

The positive qualities you need stem from the desire to achieve, which is predicated upon the BELIEF that YOU CAN achieve.

Harry Haight BELIEVES HE CAN achieve, and he is driven to prove it. To deal successfully with him, you must acquire a strong self-image, a positive faith in YOURSELF. This belief is the prerequisite to all positive motivation.

WHY DO SOME HAVE "IT," AND SOME DON'T?

Why do so many struggle through day after day with eyes downcast and hollow, minds asleep, and hearts not in their work? Why are so many parasites for security and a paycheck, and thus so easily exploited?

Why do others (few, to be sure!) ascend to the heights of achievement like human comets blazing in a sky of grey mediocrity? Where do they get their energy, their conviction, their love of life?

Is there *really* a fathomless, limitless reservoir of energy and joy within us *all*, just waiting to be unfolded?

These questions have puzzled great and noble minds for centuries. Many optimistic ideas have been expressed, and many hopeful theories have been evolved which point to the undiscovered potential of the human creature.

However, many scientists have argued that man is not the heir to the ages, but rather a helpless creature deluded by an illusion of free will, a puppet manipulated by forces beyond his control.

Years ago the remarkably creative psychologist, Abraham Maslow, studied the problem. He discovered clinically the same optimistic factors about humankind that the "positive thinkers" had intuitively claimed all along:

THERE IS, IN THE CORE OF EACH OF US, A VAST UNTAPPED POTENTIAL THAT CRIES OUT FOR EXPRESSION AND ACTUALIZATION. ONCE AN INNER CONNECTION IS MADE (AND RESOLUTELY KEPT) WITH THIS INNER CORE, WE BEGIN TO UNFOLD AND ACTUALIZE A POTENTIAL MORE VAST AND GRAND THAN OUR WILDEST IMAGINATIONS COULD POSSIBLY VISUALIZE.

Maslow discovered this intrinsic potential of human beings when he was studying healthy people – achievers and movers who were also people of compassion and warmth. These people Maslow called Self-Actualizers.

No one had broadly and seriously studied a healthy achiever before, let alone made an in-depth analysis of *hundreds* of them.

Virtually all psychiatry and much of psychology had been based upon the study of the sick, the depressing emotional cripples and losers of humankind. No wonder we had a pessimistic view of ourselves!

The next chapter deals with the amazing scientific discoveries of Abraham Maslow . . . discoveries which were offered to a world not yet entirely ready for them. These discoveries will help you reach your own inner core of potential, *in spite of your immature boss.*

AN OVERVIEW OF WHAT EACH BOSS *REALLY* BELIEVES

HARRY HAIGHT:
The Ruthless/Aggressive
Management Point of View:

ABOUT EMPLOYEES: "Employees must
be shown who is boss in no uncertain
terms. An employee cannot be trusted
to work unless the boss can put the
fear of God into him!"

ABOUT HIMSELF: "I'm a natural leader,
tough and smart! Don't give me that
stuff about this theory or that; I'm an
old warrior! People may not like me,
but they respect me for my gutsy,
decisive actions!"

MIKE MATURE:
The Compassionate/Assertive
Management Point of View:

ABOUT EMPLOYEES: "People are each
unique and individual. Each will be
motivated when he is convinced that
it is in his best interests to achieve
an objective . . . company objectives
must be tied to healthy self-interests !"

ABOUT HIMSELF: "I'm
good, but I still have a lot to learn.
I am optimistic about my ability to
grow, and to help the people around
me grow. Most people respond to
strong, positive and sensitive leadership."

FRED FRIDGIDE:
The Hostile/Timid
Management Point of View:

ABOUT PEOPLE: "Employees do
whatever they decide they want to do.
Motivational methods have no effect
on anyone. I don't trust employees,
and for good reason. I keep a low
profile in this lousy company, and I
survive. *That* is the name of the game."

ABOUT HIMSELF: "I'm a realist. Life is
tough, and no matter what I try it
turns out rotten. I avoid people; they
are no damn good!"

GARY GOODMAN:
The Warm/Timid
Management Point of View:

ABOUT PEOPLE: "People will work
hard for someone they like. I try to
make friends with my employees and
I work hard to be worthy of their
approval. I consider myself a people
expert . . it's people who matter."

ABOUT HIMSELF: "Some folks might
see me as a bit on the soft side, but
they fail to understand my expertise
is in people. This is why everyone likes
me. Having friends and being liked is
all that really counts."

WHAT EACH EMPLOYEE *REALLY* BELIEVES

THE RUTHLESS/AGGRESSIVE EMPLOYEE...

"I didn't make this rugged world, but you better believe I know how to fight for my place in it. A guy has to look out for himself, trust nobody, and never let his guard down. I'm gonna make it because I'm as good and as tough as they come. It's kill or be killed!"

THE COMPASSIONATE/ ASSERTIVE EMPLOYEE...

"Me? I'm darned capable, one of the best at what I do in my field. But I still have a lot of growing and learning to do. I am as passionate about unfolding my abilities as Harry is about winning."

THE HOSTILE/TIMID EMPLOYEE...

"This world and this company are terrible. For eighteen years I've worked my guts out and no one gives a damn. My boss is a bum, he favors other employees because they put up a phony front. One thing though, I have survived, and nobody is better at surviving than I am."

THE WARM/TIMID EMPLOYEE...

"I don't know why people disagree and fight so often; we are all good folks underneath it all. Sure, I haven't set the world on fire, but everyone likes me and I really belong. That's the important thing in life, belonging and being liked."

POINTS TO

BECAUSE YOUR BOSS BELIEVES certain things about himself and the world around him, he tends to act in one of four basic patterns: RUTHLESS/AGGRESSIVE, HOSTILE/TIMID, WARM/TIMID, or COMPASSIONATE/ASSERTIVE.

BECAUSE YOU ALSO BELIEVE certain things about yourself and the world around you, you also tend to act in one of these four basic patterns.

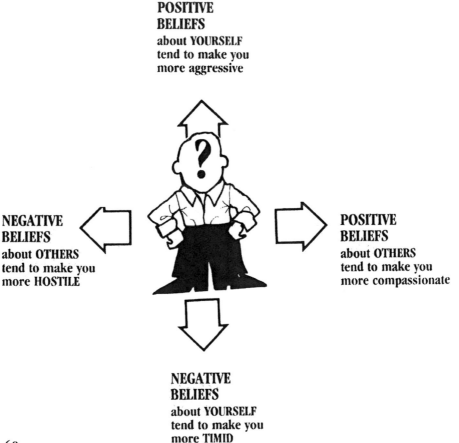

POSITIVE BELIEFS
about YOURSELF
tend to make you
more aggressive

NEGATIVE BELIEFS
about OTHERS
tend to make you
more HOSTILE

POSITIVE BELIEFS
about OTHERS
tend to make you
more compassionate

NEGATIVE BELIEFS
about YOURSELF
tend to make you
more TIMID

REMEMBER:

THE RELATIONSHIP YOU HAVE WITH YOUR BOSS depends upon what kind of an individual he is, and what kind of an individual you are. To make dramatic changes in this relationship, you must make adjustments in the one part of the relationship that you control — your own part.

REFERENCES:

V. R. Buzzota, R. E. Lefton, Manual Sherberg: EFFECTIVE SELLING THROUGH PSYCHOLOGY: DIMENSIONAL SALES AND SALES MANAGEMENT STRATEGIES, Psychological Associates, Inc. (WILEY INTERSCIENCE), St. Louis, Missouri, 1972

James David Barber: THE PRESIDENTIAL CHARACTER: PREDICTING PERFORMANCE IN THE WHITE HOUSE, Prentice-Hall, Inc., Englewood Cliffs, New Jersey, 1972

Richard J. Lowery, Editor: DOMINANCE, SELF-ESTEEM, SELF-ACTUALIZATION, THE GERMINAL PAPERS OF A. H. MASLOW, Brooks-Cole Publishing Company, Monterey, California, 1973

Colin Wilson: NEW PATHWAYS IN PSYCHOLOGY, MASLOW AND THE POST-FREUDIAN REVOLUTION, Taplinger Publishing Co., New York, 1972

Abraham Maslow: EUPSYCHIAN MANAGEMENT, MAKING GOOD MANAGEMENT BETTER, Richard D. Irwin and the Dorsey Press, Homewood, Illinois, 1965

PSYCHOLOGY TODAY — AN INTRODUCTION, CMR Books, Del Mar, California, 1970

Robert R. Blake & Jane Srygley Mouton: THE GRID FOR SALES EXCELLENCE, McGraw-Hill, New York, 1980

**THE DUMBFOUNDED PROFESSOR WATCHED AS
JOE WROTE TWO WORDS ON THE BLACKBOARD**

O NE AFTERNOON several years ago (the story goes), a great behavioral scientist was scheduled to do an evening lecture on a subject he had mastered: Human Motivation.

The lecture hall was dim and deserted as he prepared his notes, made diagrams, and wrote theorems on the several blackboards he had at his disposal.

The scientist, whom we shall call Edgar Marsh, was absorbed in his work and did not notice a side door opening and the janitor enter. Joe the janitor was carrying a bucket, a broom, and a mop.

Joe stood in the shadows and observed the great professor, who was working intently and filling up his third blackboard with comments and notes.

Interested, Joe walked down to the front and took a seat. For several minutes he watched Edgar Marsh. Then suddenly Joe asked.

"Say, are you professor Marsh?"

The great man stopped and turned. He smiled magnanimously and said, "Yes, I am. Are you familiar with my work?"

"No sir. I just knew you were speaking tonight. What are all the diagrams and notes about?"

"Well, you see here the distillation of 27 years of study, the fruits of all my research. Here before you are the fundamental elements of human motivation – that is – the great force that makes some of us great achievers, the power that drives us on."

"Hmmmm . . ." Joe murmured. He studied the boards silently.

Dr. Marsh turned back to his work and began writing again. Several minutes passed. Suddenly Joe spoke again.

"You know professor, all that stuff you are writing up there could be summed up in two words."

Slightly perturbed, the professor turned to face Joe.

"My good man! How can you make such a statement? The great minds on this planet have struggled with this problem for centuries! Vast amounts of knowledge and insights have been acquired! These words barely scratch the surface of what we know. How could you sum this up in two words?"

At this Joe got up from his seat and strode confidently up to the professor. He took the chalk from Marsh's hand and stepped over to the board. Then Joe took the eraser and erased a large area.

The dumbfounded professor watched as Joe wrote two words on the blackboard. Then he replaced the chalk, went back and picked up his mop, broom, and pail and left the auditorium.

Professor Marsh stared at the words on the board. Indeed, he admitted to himself, here were possibly the *two* most important words in the world.

When someone *had* what they described, *something happened.* These were the words that describe what motivated men like Louis Pasteur, Vince Lombardi and Mohammed Ali, as well as women like Helen Keller and Florence Nightingale. In fact, no one had ever done anything of note unless he "had" what these two words describe.

These were the words that described the difference between world class and mediocrity. Perhaps here indeed was the secret of all human motivation!

CAN YOU GUESS THOSE TWO WORDS?

4

The STARTLING "SECRET" of SENSATIONAL ACHIEVEMENT

...Why Them that Have "IT" Gets, And Them that Don't Have "IT" Lose the Little They Have

T HE "GOTTA WANNA" story has one major shortcoming. The trouble with the story is that most people don't know, (or aren't conscious of) what it is they want.

As the philosopher of MAD COMIC BOOK, Alfred E. Newman, is purported to have said: "I don't know what it is I want, but I'm pretty sure I don't have it."

The human creature is a wanting animal. And he ALWAYS wants MOST what he NEEDS MOST, or THINKS he NEEDS MOST.

About ten years ago I told the "GOTTA WANNA" story to a friend of mine named Harold Anderson. Harold had a good job, but he was very unhappy. He wanted to be his own boss.

The story inspired Harold. It inspired him so much, in fact, that he actually quit his job and went into business for himself!

Unfortunately, he only lasted about six months. His business failed and he actually went back to his old company *doing a lesser job!*

Did Harold lose his motivation?

No . . . Harold had plenty of motivation – but it was motivation for security. He was accustomed to a regular paycheck; he took it for granted. When he quit his job, his motivation for INDEPENDENCE sustained him for a while.

But, when his paychecks quit coming, the need for SECURITY reasserted itself. It soon began to overwhelm his desire for INDEPENDENCE.

Perhaps the greatest humiliation one can imagine would be to go off on one's own only to lose the incentive, and to languish and fail. And then go back to the old job! Wow! Talk about motivation! Harold had tremendous motivation – to recover his security! He was a proud man, and the experience was a terrible one.

Could Harold have avoided this disaster?

Yes – with some wise planning and preparation. If he had known what to expect, the fear thoughts and anxieties would not have overwhelmed him so suddenly. He could have been in a better position financially, less vulnerable.

As it happened, Harold's mind went into a survival mode, and he could not think about anything but survival. *He became a survival machine.*

Why are survival and security thoughts so powerful? Why do we permit them to cripple our ambitions and dim our vision?

A REMARKABLE BREAKTHROUGH

Abraham Maslow developed a "THEORY OF HUMAN MOTIVATION" and published it in 1943. It became a classic and is the foundation of behavioral science.

✳ The basic premises of Maslow's theory are simple:

(1) A human being is a "needing and wanting" animal who is never satisfied for long.

(2) A human being strives to satisfy his needs and wants.

(3) When an individual satisfies a need or want, a new need emerges.

(4) Once a need is satisfied and stays satisfied, it no longer motivates.

(5) Higher needs do not normally emerge until the lower needs are satisfied.

(6) The lower needs are more concerned with survival, the higher needs with well-being or self expression.

✳ ● Next Maslow arranged our needs and wants into groups of priorities.
- *FIRST AND STRONGEST NEED: BIOLOGICAL*
  Food, air, water, etc.
- *SECOND, AND THE NEXT STRONGEST NEED: SAFETY*
  Security, structure, predictability
- *THIRD, AND NEXT STRONGEST: LOVE AND BELONGINGNESS*
  Social needs, needs for approval, affection
- *FOURTH: SELF-ESTEEM*
  Achievement, recognition, status symbols
- *FIFTH: INDEPENDENCE*
  Control, autonomy, power
- *SIXTH: SELF-ACTUALIZATION*
  Development, growth, self-improvement

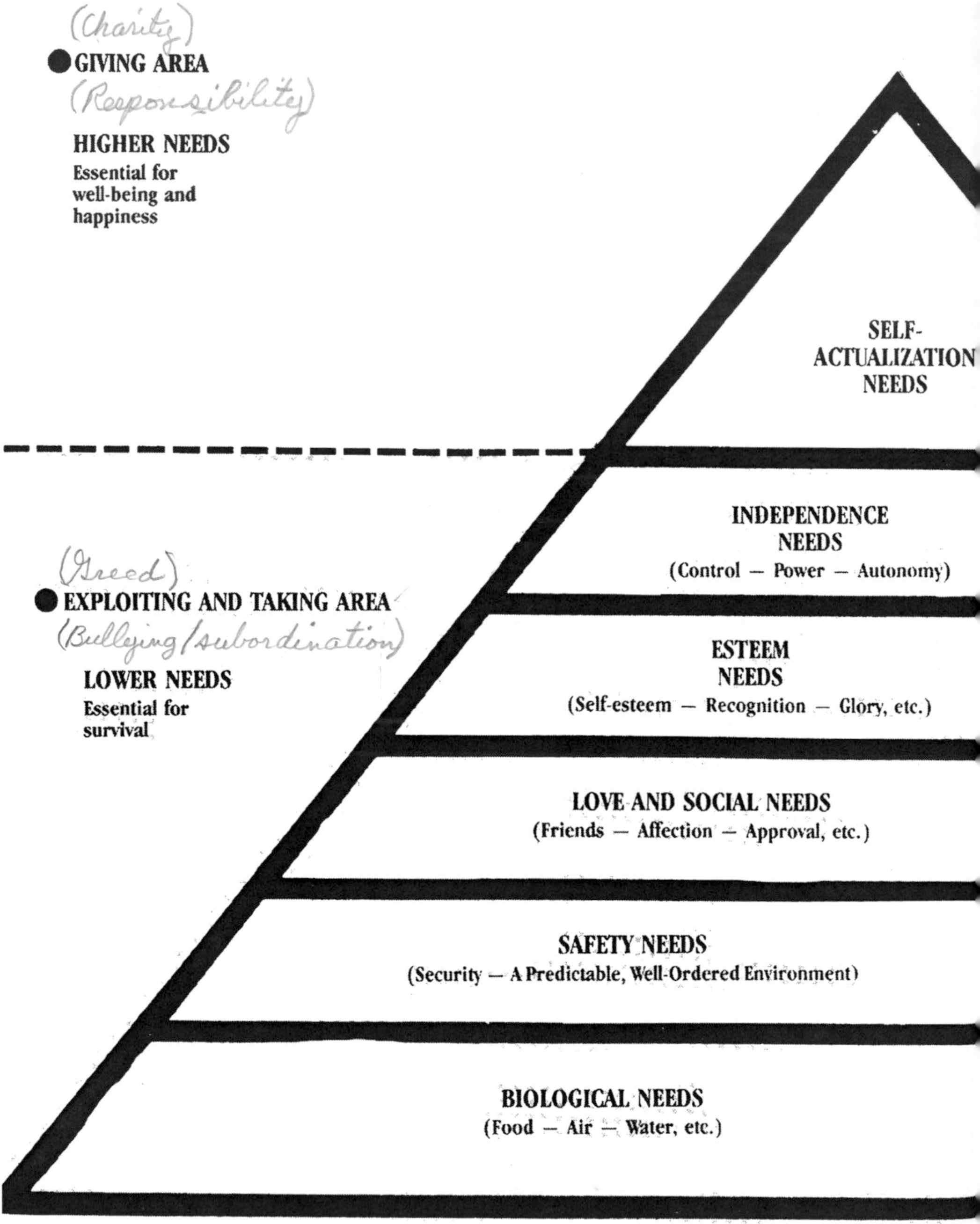

(Charity)

● **GIVING AREA**

(Responsibility)

HIGHER NEEDS
Essential for
well-being and
happiness

**SELF-
ACTUALIZATION
NEEDS**

(Greed)

● **EXPLOITING AND TAKING AREA**

(Bullying / subordination)

LOWER NEEDS
Essential for
survival

**INDEPENDENCE
NEEDS**
(Control — Power — Autonomy)

**ESTEEM
NEEDS**
(Self-esteem — Recognition — Glory, etc.)

LOVE AND SOCIAL NEEDS
(Friends — Affection — Approval, etc.)

SAFETY NEEDS
(Security — A Predictable, Well-Ordered Environment)

BIOLOGICAL NEEDS
(Food — Air — Water, etc.)

Maslow arranged these needs in a pyramid, with the stronger basic needs as the foundation, and each of the other needs following up to the apex.

WE ARE ALWAYS MOTIVATED. WE ARE ALWAYS STRIVING. Being motivated is as natural as breathing.

Maslow's remarkable pyramid explains how our inner needs work, one after another, to "pull our strings" and cause us to behave as we do.

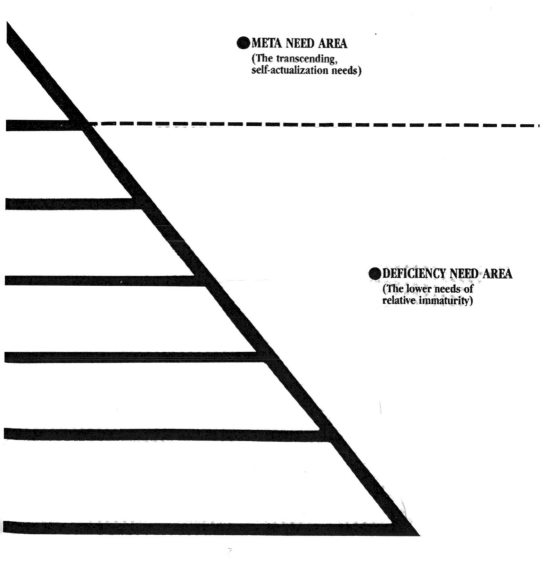

●META NEED AREA
(The transcending,
self-actualization needs)

●DEFICIENCY NEED AREA
(The lower needs of
relative immaturity)

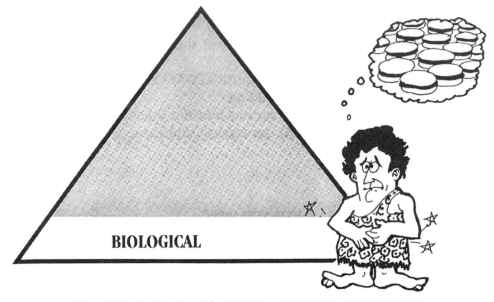

THE HUNGRY INDIVIDUAL'S UTOPIA: UNLIMITED HAMBURGERS

A human's first needs are biological survival. When a creature is hungry or thirsty or cannot breathe, it cannot think of anything but survival. He will disregard his own safety if hungry enough.

These urges for food, water, air and so on are overwhelmingly powerful. ONCE THEY ARE FAIRLY WELL SATISFIED, A NEW SET OF NEEDS BEGIN TO EMERGE, THE NEEDS FOR SAFETY AND SECURITY . . .

SAFETY

(BIOLOGICAL NEEDS now generally satisfied, no longer motivate)

THE FRIGHTENED INDIVIDUAL'S UTOPIA: SAFETY AND SECURITY

After biological needs, the next needs to emerge are the needs for security, safety and order.

Even if a mature individual should suddenly lose his job, he would move to re-establish his security above all other things. Once re-established, the individual would become "himself" again. WHEN THE SAFETY AND SECURITY NEEDS BEGIN TO BE SATISFIED, THEY NO LONGER MOTIVATE AND A NEW NEED EMERGES...

GEE... I'M LONELY!

THE LONELY INDIVIDUAL'S UTOPIA: LOTS OF FRIENDS, LOVE AND APPROVAL

After a human being satisfies his biological, safety and security needs, his love and belongingness, and social needs emerge. He wants friends, family, companions and affectionate approval. ONCE THE LOVE AND BELONGING NEEDS ARE GENERALLY SATISFIED, A NEW NEED BEGINS TO MOTIVATE THE HUMAN CREATURE...

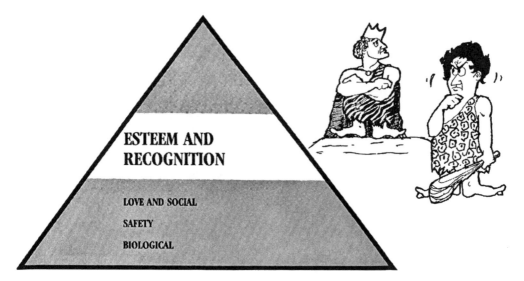

THE SELF-DOUBTING INDIVIDUAL'S UTOPIA: ESTEEM AND RECOGNITION

A human being, other needs satisfied, begins to want to achieve or validate his self-esteem. He wants "ego food," symbols of achievement, status symbols.

WHEN THE NEED FOR ESTEEM AND RECOGNITION BEGINS TO BE SATISFIED, THERE EMERGES A NEED FOR INDEPENDENCE AND POWER, AND AUTONOMY...

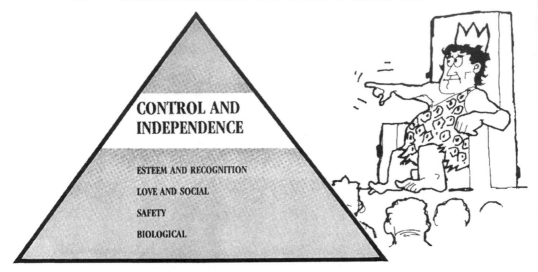

THE POWER-HUNGRY INDIVIDUAL'S UTOPIA: CONTROL AND INDEPENDENCE

Independence needs are closely related to esteem needs, but they extend further. At this point an individual desires to control the destinies of others as well as his own; he craves power and strives to prove that he needs no other person.

ONCE THESE NEEDS FOR CONTROL AND INDEPENDENCE BEGIN TO BE SATISFIED, THE NEEDS FOR SELF-ACTUALIZATION BEGIN TO EMERGE ...

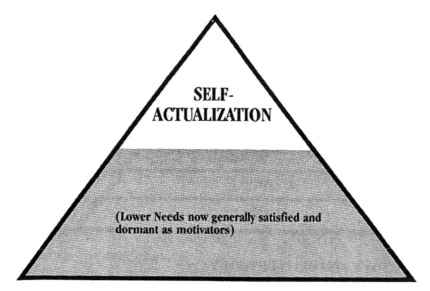

SELF-
ACTUALIZATION

(Lower Needs now generally satisfied and
dormant as motivators)

THE MATURE INDIVIDUAL'S UTOPIA: THE PROCESS OF SELF- ACTUALIZATION

As the human begins to satisfy and transcend all the other needs, there begins to gradually emerge the needs for self-actualization, the meta needs (or transcendent needs). A whole new set of rules apply to the self-actualization process.

First, the process is unending; the desire to fulfill one's potential is never satisfied. It is a PROCESS, not a destination.

Next, self-actualization is a process of actually *putting something back* into the world. All the other needs are satisfied by *taking something* that the individual needs: First material things, then ego food, love, esteem and power.

As a child we learn to seek material survival. Then we learn to seek love. The process of maturity is learning to quit seeking love and approval and begin seeking *to* love instead. Maturity is, in fact, the process that permits the individual to give love.

Virtually every ugly and unpleasant thing individuals do is really the act of TRYING TO BE LOVED rather than TRYING TO LOVE. Love is the limitless commodity that is made rare by the immaturity of the human race.

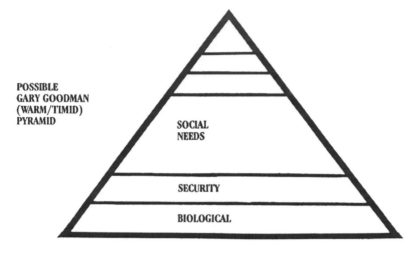

POSSIBLE
GARY GOODMAN
(WARM/TIMID)
PYRAMID

EACH PERSON'S PYRAMID IS DIFFERENT

Of course, no two human beings are exactly alike. Each individual's personal "pyramid" will be different from all others. Occasionally there will be an inversion of needs (for example, an unusual individual might crave self-expression more than food!). Each need blends into, rather than is clearly delineated from, its most closely related needs.

Here are two pyramids. Each is for a different individual. One individual is addicted to social needs. The other is addicted to ego food. (Approval hardly interests a Harry Haight type of person at all.)

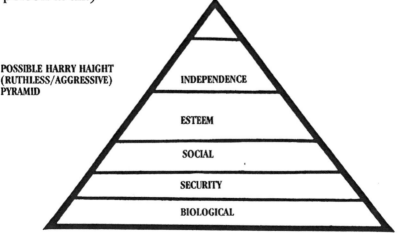

POSSIBLE HARRY HAIGHT
(RUTHLESS/AGGRESSIVE)
PYRAMID

THE AMAZING "MOUNTAIN" OF MOTIVATION

Imagine a towering mountain. At the summit is an area of "self-actualization," the land of the world-class individual, the supreme achiever. As we look closer, we see that the rest of this mountain is populated with billions of people.

Barely ½ of 1% of the total number of people are at the summit. In the areas represented by aggressive achievers, the independence and self-esteem areas, less than five percent of the total number of people exist.

95% of the human race is on the rest of the mountain, striving for approval, social status, safety, and – of course – many are striving simply to survive.

As we look at this mountain we can see why so few have made it to the top. The lower regions are much warmer and more comfortable. In the lower regions there are many more places to hide, places to enjoy at least a superficial companionship lacking in the higher regions of the mountain.

As we observe the teeming billions on this mountain we note that there is a tumultuous struggle going on. Many people are apparently trying to make progress toward the summit, but are actually simply going in circles.

Upon this mountain we place our bosses. FRED FRIDGIDE seeks to fulfill his needs for SECURITY AND SAFETY. GARY GOODMAN has security needs to a lesser degree, and most wants SOCIAL CONTACTS and APPROVAL. HARRY HAIGHT has tremendous drives for ESTEEM, POWER, for GLORY, and for CONTROL. MIKE MATURE is emerging from the needs for independence and control into the SELF-ACTUALIZING AREAS.

Those employees and bosses who have "IT" (INITIATIVE) grab the lion's share of the material riches, and the credit, and glory.

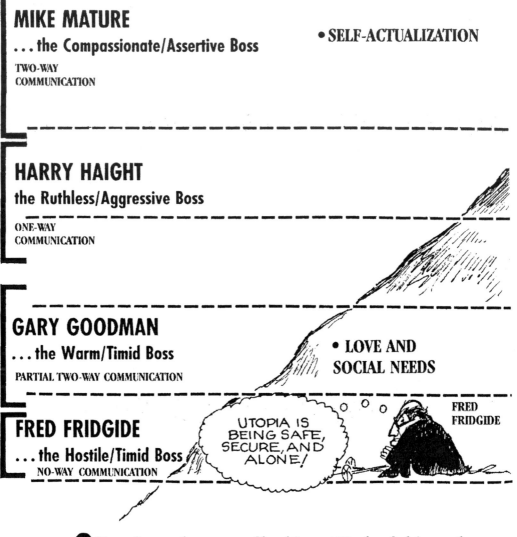

MIKE MATURE
...the Compassionate/Assertive Boss

TWO-WAY
COMMUNICATION

• SELF-ACTUALIZATION

HARRY HAIGHT
the Ruthless/Aggressive Boss

ONE-WAY
COMMUNICATION

GARY GOODMAN
...the Warm/Timid Boss

PARTIAL TWO-WAY COMMUNICATION

• LOVE AND
SOCIAL NEEDS

FRED FRIDGIDE
...the Hostile/Timid Boss
NO-WAY COMMUNICATION

UTOPIA IS
BEING SAFE,
SECURE, AND
ALONE!

FRED
FRIDGIDE

● Here is another way of looking at Maslow's hierarchy
of needs! Note where each boss has been placed in
the illustration. Take a few minutes to get a good
understanding of this concept. Keep a mental image
of it, you'll find it valuable!

MOUNTAIN OF MOTIVATION...

THE SIMPLE ART OF CONTROLLING PRISONERS OF WAR

During the Korean War, there were virtually no American escapes from captivity. This was astonishing, because the Chinese and North Korean POW camps were not all that escape-proof.

Later we were to learn how the Chinese and North Koreans did it.

When a group of American and UN POW's were brought into a camp for confinement, they were carefully observed for several days. Aggressive, assertive types were identified and singled out.

About one man in twenty seemed to have "IT" . . . that is, enough initiative to cause trouble. Five percent, in other words, were "dangerous."

These five percent were simply removed from the rest of the prisoners and placed in maximum security.

The remaining 95% were passive enough and easy to handle. Few even tried to escape.

This story illustrates the world's lack of aggressive, assertive "doers" and leaders. The world must draw upon the small percentage of aggressive people available for leadership roles.

And, of these assertive individuals, only a tiny fraction are truly mature, self-actualizing people! *The rest of the 5% are assertive enough, but are to some degree ruthless and hostile!*

No wonder there are so many "Harry Haight" bosses in the world!

YOU PROBABLY ARE TOO PASSIVE

Most people who study this material are sensitive and considerate enough of others . . . and these are *important qualities to retain.* But most of the sensitive people in the world lack calm, resolute assertiveness and initiative.

In other words, it is possible that you may be too concerned with taking love and approval from the world, or in establishing safety and security. This makes you vulnerable to the Harry Haight type of exploiter.

We can see how it would be relatively simple for Harry to control and manipulate employees addicted to security and approval. Harry makes security and approval rare "commodities" by keeping people insecure and in anxiety about their perfor- mance.   Harry controls by withholding approval and losing his temper to intimidate and get his way.

But you are ready to learn to handle this most difficult of all immature personalities. Harry has emotional needs also, and these needs "pull his strings" just as surely as your own inner needs pull yours.

Let's see inside the REAL Harry Haight. Let's see how this mighty man is really a puppet acting out the role of a fearless macho leader . . . and how he is really a terror-filled individual on a tightrope – running faster and faster – afraid that if he stops, or hesitates, or shows weakness or indecision, he will fall and be destroyed.

POINTS TO REMEMBER:

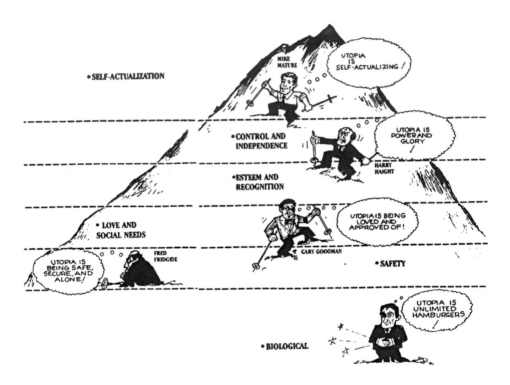

REMEMBER THE AMAZING MOUNTAIN OF MOTIVATION...

Note where your own boss is, and also where you tend to be.
For now, observe the interplay of needs, yours <u>and</u> his.

REFERENCES:

Abraham Maslow: <u>MOTIVATION and PERSONALITY</u>, Harper and Row, New York, 1954

Abraham Maslow: <u>THE FARTHER REACHES OF HUMAN NATURE</u>, The Viking Press, New York, 1971

Buzzotta, Lefton & Sherberg: <u>EFFECTIVE SELLING THROUGH PSYCHOLOGY: DIMENSIONAL SALES AND SALES MANAGEMENT STRATEGIES</u>, Wiley Interscience, New York, 1972

James Barber: <u>THE PRESIDENTIAL CHARACTER: PREDICTING PERFORMANCE IN THE WHITE HOUSE</u>, Prentice-Hall Inc., Englewood Cliffs, New Jersey, 1972

Manuel J. Smith: <u>WHEN I SAY NO, I FEEL GUILTY</u>, Dial Press, New York, 1975

W. Hugh Missildine: <u>YOUR INNER CHILD OF THE PAST</u>, Simon and Schuster, New York, 1963

Robert R. Blake & Jane Srygley Mouton: <u>THE GRID FOR SALES EXCELLENCE</u>, McGraw-Hill, New York, 1980

Robert R. Blake & Jane Srygley Mouton: <u>THE VERSATILE MANAGER</u>, Dow-Jones Irwin, Homewood, Illinois, 1978

Thomas L. Quick: <u>THE QUICK MOTIVATION METHOD</u>, St. Martin's Press, New York, 1980

PART III

THE BOSSES...

The Incredible Truth About What They REALLY Think About Employees, and What Their Employees REALLY Think About Them...

"THROW THIS BOOK AWAY! GET TOUGH! BE BRUTAL! GET THEM BEFORE THEY GET YOU!!"

Y OU ARE ushered into the palatial office of Harry Haight for a candid interview. Harry speaks:

"Sit down. It's time for some plain talk!

"The last thing this world needs is a book like the one you are reading to stir people up. All those theories about managing people are baloney. I'm a natural leader; I have charisma. I've always had charisma.

"I've succeeded in my own business – and that's what counts – results. Some egghead who hasn't fought the battles and paid his dues knows nothing about winning.

"Yes, it's obvious that I'm a tough guy. I am a realist. I simply see things the way they are – not the way, maybe, they should be.

"Everybody is out to get his own – it's kill or be killed. Employees are by nature lazy; they only work when they are intimidated into it. This is my strength, I scare the hell out of 'em! Ha!

"Sure we have turnover – it's a weeding out process. The weaklings fall to the side ... it's king of the hill. And by the way – I'm the king.

"Yeah, I make them toe the line with some pretty demanding regulations. Nobody gets away with anything in this company! But people must have strict regulations ... they need them.

"My employees also need me. I'm dynamic, brilliant, and I can do more work in an hour than any of them can do in a couple of days.

"All the innovations and creative ideas come out of this office. All the critical planning must be done by me ... ALONE. The big problem is to get the troops to try to understand the deep meanings of my thinking ... so I insist that they are not to think on their own – they are to EXECUTE.

"Yes, I make the decisions. The results speak for themselves. Last year two of our competitors in Cleveland went broke – belly up! THAT'S what I call results!

"Management in this company is doing it my way, everytime. They listen – they don't talk back. They know who the boss is ... and if they don't produce – it's out!"

When you clear your throat, Harry leaps to his feet, "No! Don't say anything! Just listen a minute!"

He continues: "Look around the company here. Look at the employees. I am strong; they are weak and undependable. I'm self-motivated; they work only when their security is threatened.

"Yes, I know all about that Maslow rectangle! That one you read about in the last chapter. I studied it for years. In fact I wrote an award-winning paper on it when I went to Yale.

"Remember, I'm the guy who MUST succeed. There are a lot of guys who are after our company and some members of the Board of Directors who would like to see me replaced ... they're jealous.

"Harry Haight is one cool poker player though; I can outlast all of them. Everyone will learn that you don't cross me and live to tell about it.

"Look at it this way. If it wasn't for me, and the few who are like me, nothing would ever get done. Most people are timid weaklings, afraid of their own shadows . . . they'd be lost without men like me.

"Now! While you are here, I have a three-hour video tape of me giving a motivation talk to my managers. I take the hide off of them!

"Just sit back and listen and you'll get the full impact of *my own* management ideas . . ."

"I TAKE THE HIDE OFF OF 'EM!"

HARRY HAIGHT...
The Ruthless/
Aggressive Boss

**...How He Rules with Brutal Intimidation...and
How to Master the Skillful Art of Handling Him**

A S YOU leave Harry Haight's office, you prepare to keep the
four additional interviews that have been arranged for you.
These are interviews with the employee-managers who have the
closest contact with Harry Haight.

Your first interview is with Harry's current Number 1 Man,
Ned Nasty. Like Harry, Ned is a Ruthless/Aggressive personality.
But, as you will see, Ned is not in a position to talk quite as
freely as Harry. (Even though you promised confidentiality, Ned
is very suspicious.)

NED BEGINS TO TALK LOUDLY INTO HIS LAMP . . .

HARRY HAIGHT . . . AS SEEN THROUGH THE EYES OF NED NASTY

"OK, I've got just a few minutes. Harry wants me to fly to Cleveland and fire the Manager of the branch there. Got a little too big for his britches . . . Having an affair with his secretary, too. That is against company policy! But the thing that really finished this guy was when Harry found out he made fun of Harry's bad breath! Wow! THAT made Harry mad!

"You know, that hot-shot in Cleveland was after my job! That's why I told Harry what he said about his breath. I'm a tough competitor! Staying on top of the hill takes a real fighter.

"Now about Harry. He is a great man, a mover, a shaker. He's as unyielding and resolute as any man I know. He is, in fact, a genius.

"Which is why he picked me. He needs a right hand man every bit as tough and as smart as he is. In all modesty, I can't think of anyone who could fill the bill better than me.

"I'm called the enforcer . . . sometimes the night stalker. Ha! Why they're more afraid of me than Harry! I weed 'em out quick!"

Ned Nasty suddenly walks around his desk and begins to talk loudly into his lamp, as though it were a microphone.

"But it would be wrong to say that anyone could match Harry! No sir! Harry is the toughest, most rugged, most dynamic man in the world. I love the man!"

Then Ned turns on the radio near the lamp and leads you over to a window. He speaks in soft tones.

"Now, confidentially though, Harry is beginning to slip. He's getting old . . . losing some of the biting edge. I'm probably the man who will be taking over this place before long."

Ned looks around.

"Frankly, I think senility is beginning to creep in. He chews me out too damn much, makes me feel like a dog. And I do all the work! Every creative idea this company produces starts right here!

"Yeah, he pays well. He has to. To put up with Harry I deserve twice the pay I'm getting.

"Ned Nasty is no stooge, though. I've got some pretty good irons in the fire. Some companies would pay a lot for me and what I know about this company!

"You know. You got to look after Number One. It's kill or be killed!"

Ned leads you over to the lamp again. With a wink he says loudly: "To sum up, let me say that Harry Haight may very well go down in history . . . in fact, if things had been a little different Harry could have become president . . . President of the United States! He'd have been a great one!"

You leave Ned Nasty's office and make your way down the hall to a remote, dismal part of the building. Here you find the small office of Charlie Colder, the Hostile/Timid accountant. Charlie is at first reluctant to talk, but gradually he loosens up a bit as he develops more trust in you.

"I'M TRAPPED,"
SAYS CHARLIE

HARRY HAIGHT AS SEEN THROUGH THE EYES OF CHARLIE COLDER

"Yes, I've been here 11 years," Charlie explains. "I'm staying on, what choice do I have? I'm trapped.

"Life is dismal – I try to make the best of the rotten hand I was dealt. Harry is a despicable tyrant, but after all, he didn't create this crummy world.

"Me, I stay out of Harry's way. All I want is to be left alone and have no one interfere with my job.

"Would you believe – I'm the only manager here with a college degree? Harry didn't even graduate from Junior High School! Oh yeah, he went to Yale for a two-week symposium...and so Harry tells people 'when I went to Yale...'

"They all make mistakes in grammar and know nothing about proper financial management. But...let them have their fun, I just want to be left alone...I keep a low profile. That's how I survive!

"I know Ned and Harry probably told you a lot about me. I know they think I'm too passive. But I've seen plenty of Ned Nastys come and go – and I'm still here! Survival is all that matters, and I'm a master at it.

"I stick to the rules and pass them on – even when I know they are wrong. I'm no hero; let them find out for themselves. That way they can't blame me – I did what I was told.

"Harry, and Ned too, violate every single regulation we have. They make up their own rules. Then they fire someone for any minor infraction.

"Harry actually had the nepotism rule written out of the company manual to make it a 'top management prerogative,' then he hired his son to work in the Seattle branch. He also fired a guy for having a part-time job, yet Harry owns a company privately that does business with us and makes him a bundle of dough with sweetheart deals.

"Ned has some deals going too. He has a lot of girl friends and he flies them on pleasure trips using the company plane and his company credit card. Harry just looks the other way.

"But what do I care? If I left and went somewhere else things would probably be worse.

"So I stick it out and survive. Isn't that what life is all about?"

HARRY HAIGHT AS SEEN THROUGH THE EYES OF SAM SWEETER

Your next stop is the maintenance area, and the head mechanic, good old Sam Sweeter, a Warm/Timid individual.

You have a difficult time getting Sam to stick to the subject. He digresses to a million other things. He just loves to talk and talk. So we present his remarks in greatly edited form.

"Hello! How wonderful of you to come visit us! My name is Sam Sweeter, and you are welcome. We are just one big happy family in this company!

"Well, Harry Haight is deep-down a good and sensitive man. He is pressured very hard though, and sometimes it shows.

"Sometimes Harry is a tiny bit unreasonable...but he never means to be. He is a human being, and human beings are sometimes less than considerate.

"Oh, I admit that it hurt a bit when I found my Christmas card to him in the waste basket...the one with my whole family on the front, holding up the huge model of the company trademark I made in my shop. I thought he would want to keep it.

"I ADMIT IT HURT WHEN I
FOUND MY CHRISTMAS CARD
TO HIM IN THE WASTE BASKET . . ."

"And then Harry forgot that I had worked night and day, on my own time too, to develop the new maintenance system that saved the company $158,000 last year. He told the board of directors that it was his idea . . . but I think he really believed it was, after a while . . .

"Harry did give me a fifty dollar bonus for the idea, and that shows his heart is in the right place.

"Harry just pushes too hard, he needs to slow down and smell the roses along the way. I told him this once and I guess I picked the wrong time because he really chewed me out . . .

"Harry thinks I'm too easy-going. But I love this job. I love the people here . . . we are all on the same team.

"People are the important thing. See, I'm way behind in my maintenance procedure because I took time to talk to you. But that's OK, because you're people! Get it?

"But to understand me, you need to know about my family, my dogs, and how we live our lives . . . then you'll learn to like me as I like you . . .

"In fact I have some home movies here . . . the trucks can wait. I'd love to show you some scenes of my little son Clarence and his pet snake farm . . ."

Our final stop is at the desk of Al Actualizer . . . a relatively new manager who is in charge of Data Processing.

HARRY HAIGHT...AS SEEN THROUGH THE EYES OF AL ACTUALIZER

The first thing you notice about Al is that his desk is neat; he seems in control of things.

Al greets you promptly on time...even though you had to change your appointment because Sam Sweeter wouldn't let you go until you'd talked to his new baby grandson on the phone.

Al seems warm and confident, a typical Compassionate/Assertive type. His eyes smile and he seems deeply interested in you. Al explains his views on Harry:

"Harry Haight is a remarkable man. He is a kind of living monument to what sheer will and indomitable courage can do in creating a material empire.

"Harry and I respect each other...I admire his ability, his guts and his initiative.

"However, I do NOT admire Harry's ruthless and thoughtless tactics. He is a psychological bully, not really much different from a bar bully. The only difference, in fact, is that Harry bullies people mentally, not physically.

"Harry is bright enough to do things straight, but he just can't resist being crafty and manipulative.

"There is but one criteria for Harry — if a proposal boosts his ego or makes him money the idea is a good one...if not, it is suspect.

"Of course, I'm paid to do a job here and I do a good one for my own self-satisfaction. I love my work.

"Frankly though, I feel blocked here. Harry won't let me create anything or innovate anything. He confines me to a limited area of operation, when I could do so much more.

"Harry loves to shoot from the hip and destroy our hard-to-come-by programs and ideas.

"But I have no personal hard feelings. I simply must plan and run my life as pragmatically as Harry runs his company. In fact, I just received a good offer from a fine company.

"I want to give Harry notice but I know he'll simply spite himself and tell me to clean out my desk immediately. That's how they do it here, so I'll plan accordingly.

"HE IS A PSYCHOLOGICAL BULLY . . ."

"The big problem is that the differences in my value system and Harry's are simply too great. I guess no one handles Harry better than I do though.

"Harry is really a piece of cake...as predictable as anybody you'll ever meet..."

As you leave Harry's building, you run into him again. He is red-faced and angry.

"What is this? Rick Ruthless tells me you are interviewing my employees! Who authorized this?"

You tell Harry that you cleared it with Ned Nasty.

"Ned Nasty! That idiot! This is the last straw for Mr. Nasty!" Harry turns to speak to the man beside him, Rick Ruthless. "Rick, call Cleveland and leave a message for Ned to get back here immediately! And Rick...you can dust off Ned's chair for yourself, tiger!"

Harry turns toward you again. "As for you, get out of here! No one is authorized to give opinions around here but me! Get out and never come back!"

And so your visit to the Harry Haight Company comes to an end. You have learned much about the way Harry looks at things, and the way he sees himself. You've learned a good deal about the way his employees see Harry.

But, what is the *real* Harry Haight like?

HARRY IS LIKE A MAN ON A LOG ROLL...

THE REAL HARRY HAIGHT... THE MAN NO ONE KNOWS

In reality, Harry is not so tough as he would like you to think. In reality, he is a deeply troubled man.

Harry is sincere when he says he sees the world as a dangerous place. He believes that people are as hostile toward him as he is to them – but he "knows" most people are afraid to show their fangs.

Harry encounters few people as assertive and fearless as he *appears* to be, so he presumes that most of the world is easy to bully – *if he shows who is boss.*

Harry Haight is like a man on a log roll; he keeps running faster and faster, the log keeps spinning faster and faster, and he has to keep going or he'll fall into the water. He has no choice, because the water is full of sharks just waiting for him to slip.

Oh, he could sit down and hold onto the log for dear life (the way Charlie Colder does), but this would be unmanly. He could ask for help, but this would show weakness.

No, Harry must keep the facade up at all costs. He must always appear decisive, positive, confident, never in doubt. He cannot admit, even to himself, the dread and emptiness he feels deep within.

One thing for sure – Harry never really laughs at himself. If there is a single sign of a man in serious trouble, it is one who no longer can laugh at his own foibles.

As Werner Erhard once pointed out: *Enlightenment means to lighten up.*

EIGHT POSITIVE TACTICS FOR HANDLING HARRY HAIGHT

The following pages will provide you with several proven and potent TACTICS for dealing with the Ruthless/Aggressive personality. These tactics give a kind of "instant" relief.

For the long run, however, tactics will not do it all for you. You must also develop a MASTER STRATEGY in order to fully neutralize the effects of poor management.

The difference between TACTICS for immediate help, and a MASTER STRATEGY for long range benefits, can be explained in this way:

When a professional football team plans a game, an overall "game plan" is developed. This is their Master Strategy, an over-view of how they will play the whole game. The team plans both defense and offense according to this overall Master Strategy.

The individual *plays* the team uses during the game to achieve its long range Master Strategy are "tactics." A team cannot usually win with a good Master Strategy and poor plays, nor can it usually win with fabulous plays and a poor Master Strategy.

The last part of this book will give 5 steps to help you create an individualized Master Strategy for the thrilling and productive life you are going to have.

For now we are going to work on your individual "plays," or your TACTICS. It's fun. And, if you apply them diligently and learn from your mistakes, you'll be in great shape to develop and apply the Master Strategy that we will later help you create.

We are going to present you with the cream of the best known tactics for dealing with Harry Haight. Begin to USE THEM IM-MEDIATELY.

TACTIC #1: KEEP COOL AND NEVER, NEVER LET HARRY PROVOKE OR INTIMIDATE YOU INTO AN ARGUMENT ... NEVER BE DEFENSIVE.

Harry is in his area of expertise when he argues ... and he is very effective at it. Further, he can be arbitrary and unreasonable if he has half an excuse, and you cannot.

TACTIC #2: LISTEN! LISTEN! LISTEN! ACTIVELY LISTEN TO WHAT HARRY IS SAYING AND HOW HE IS SAYING IT.

Active listening is tremendously effective in dealing with Harry – his ego loves it. Actually it is a rare experience for Harry to have someone REALLY listen to him; most people are too intimidated to ACTIVELY listen to him.

Active listening shows that you RESPECT Harry's ideas, and he needs this badly. You listen WITHOUT COMMENT and remember *you are not necessarily agreeing with him.* You are simply granting him the right to give his opinion. Here are several tactical rules for *active listening,* most of which were developed by Dr. Carl Rodgers:

1 Ask occasional questions during pauses ... probe with questions to determine what Harry is trying to communicate. Convey that you understand and accept Harry's feelings. (Not necessarily that you agree with them.)

2 Don't let wild, irrelevant remarks go by ... *show you are listening* by calmly probing with questions Harry's irrational and tangential asides.

3 Never interrupt or comment while Harry is in high gear. LISTEN! If he says something wrong, eventually ask for clarification. WHEN he gives clarification, simply KNIT YOUR BROW in deep concern and imply by your manner that you are intently concentrating on his statements.

4 At appropriate lulls, summarize for Harry. Show you understand and have listened carefully by saying, "I think I see what you mean. You are saying that ... (repeat his comments) ... Is that correct?"

$\underline{5}$ When and if Harry slows down and appears to be receptive, make your own comments honestly and frankly. You want to move Harry into a constructive problem-solving mode. Don't ramble or beat around the bush. State your point of view. Then SHUT UP. Let Harry speak next. NEVER speak before he does – it shows uncertainty, and the first man who speaks *loses*.

$\underline{6}$ If Harry's comment upon your position is evasive you are perfectly correct if you ask him to summarize what you just said. Of course you must do this carefully, something like this: "Mr. Haight, I guess I failed to make my statement clear. What do you think I was trying to say?"

#3: TACTICS AGAINST THE TEMPER TANTRUM

When Harry really goes berserk, some special techniques are needed. Use all of the above ACTIVE LISTENING TECHNIQUES, plus a few of these EMERGENCY TACTICS:

REMEMBER that Harry WANTS to blow up. LET HIM. Help him – encourage him! That's right! After his first wave of anger, ask for more!

> "I understand why you're angry! What else happened?"
> "Could you tell me any more about it?"
> "I did? My God, no wonder you are angry!"

The idea is to use the old complaint department trick: TALK HIM TIRED. If he starts to run down, help him get off again:

> "They don't know who they're dealing with, do they?"
> "They must think you're a pussy cat!"
> "They picked the wrong guy to cross this time, didn't they?"

– STARE at Harry's mouth. This works like magic. Listen attentively, but stare at his mouth if he gets especially abusive.

– USE the "Columbo" technique. When Harry has made an unfair and violent attack on you, you may handle it this way, *provided you have the facts:*

You start to leave, looking very defeated. Then at the last moment you pause. "Mr. Haight", you say, looking confused, "there is just one thing I don't understand."

You will be surprised about how gently he will reply, something like: "Yes, what is it?"

"Well, sir...(example) if, as you say, the production level I have achieved is poor, how is it that I've surpassed the average in my job area for the last 5 years by 32%? I know that there is something I'm overlooking, but maybe you could explain it to me..."

Harry will probably bluster a bit, but if you have your facts right he will respect you for standing up to him, even in this indirect way. Also, you did it in a manner that he could not take as a threat.

TACTIC #4: QUESTION! QUESTION! QUESTION!

We have already discussed this probing-question technique, but remember that at all times probing is effective and valuable.

Probe Harry's statements; ask for additional information.. show you are listening and want to know more.

TACTIC #5: HAVE THE FACTS! KNOW THE FACTS!

Nothing succeeds with Harry like knowing what you are talking about. And nothing will bring out his fangs faster than an unsupported and unwarranted assertion.

Any statement you make must be supported by cold, hard facts. Harry is very suspicious of unsupported, empty claims, since he himself is so often guilty of making them. Don't ever attempt to use the same tactics with him!

Harry loves charts, pictures, graphs and similar data...the more the better. Be sure, though, that they are accurate and significant!

TACTIC #6: BE FIRM — DON'T CAPITULATE! HARRY HATES QUITTERS!

Unless you have made some terrible mistake and must ask for mercy, don't ask for mercy! Harry cannot stand weak, passive people. He respects confidence and strength.

Once in a while say: "In my opinion " or "In my judgment." Your use of the word "my" (or "I") shows confidence.

Hang in, quietly, patiently. Stick to your guns. Most important, if you must one day leave Harry's employ and go somewhere more appropriate to your own values and maturity, do so *at your own convenience.*
NEVER, NEVER LOSE YOUR COOL. IT NEVER PAYS.

TACTIC #7: HOW TO HANDLE SARCASTIC BARBS

Harry will often attack strong people in a different way . . . by little nasty barbs, especially around an audience. Most often these remarks are made in a "kidding" way, but Harry is *not* kidding. Harry usually does this needling at a time when it seems socially inappropriate for you to respond.

This type of aggression is effective only if the victim is intimidated by the presence of other people – by social convention. If you are on the receiving end of this type of aggression you will likely have the impulse to smile and shrug off the remark.

Avoid the desire to go along with the interaction in a passive way, avoid the "peace at any price" temptation. You must challenge such snipes or you will be the victim over and over again. You must let Harry know that you have coldly noted his aggression.

This is difficult, because you cannot put Harry in the position of being challenged in front of others. On the other hand, you must interrupt the interaction.

There are two relatively safe ways to do this. One is to simply probe his casual remark with cool curiosity. This is effective *if* you have strong data to refute his statement. Your probe might go: "I don't understand why you said THAT, Mr. Haight. Our last job was 30% below the average cost of prior jobs. Are you kidding?"

Don't be afraid to challenge a totally false and unfair barb with factual data. Do it once or twice and Harry will avoid testing you again.

If Harry's remark is simply some kind of a nasty, unanswerable snide, you still must react, and not by smiling and shrugging it off. DON'T SMILE if you think the remark is uncalled for.

The only effective alternative is to use the cold pause and the iceberg stare. Simply stop and stare frankly at Harry (instead of staring at your feet). Then, purposefully *break off* the stare and perform some physical act. Move some object with authority, crisply organize your papers, or some other positive, *confident* action. It doesn't matter if the action has specific meaning, simply that it is performed with an air of confidence.

These three actions, the cold pause, the bold stare and the confident action should effectively break the interaction. After a few attempts to intimidate you in front of others, Harry will probably begin looking for easier prey.

TACTIC #8: THE CONTROL INITIATIVE

Harry is a *control* person . . . he will seek to keep you under control by knowing at all times *what* you are doing and *why*. This is a deep-seated need in Harry and has nothing to do with you as an individual.

To avoid being put on the defensive, keep Harry informed. Plan your work, chart out your schedules, keep accurate cost records. Send Harry informative memos *before* he asks for them.

Remember that *delay* of unpleasant communications is by no means *avoidance*. Being on top of things is a good business discipline and will greatly reduce tension in your relationship with Harry.

THE MASKS
OF HARRY HAIGHT

Harry is actually a con man at heart. He can be as charming and sweet as anyone *when he needs to be*. When Harry must use manipulative tactics, he does so with great gusto.

When Harry is manipulating someone, he deliberately uses what is called a MASK TACTIC. He usually acts the role of the good guy, Mike Mature or Gary Goodman.

Once a fellow contacted me and asked me to market some beach front lots for him. He offered me a remarkable amount of money for doing it. We'll call him Scott.

The preliminary work for Scott took several months to complete. We had many meetings, and Scott handled all the problems that came up with maturity and finesse.

He loved my work and heaped praise on me. The project went splendidly; sales were terrific. The only problem was that Scott had made a serious error on cost estimates, and wasn't making much money.

As the time drew near for me to be paid, Scott began to change dramatically. He went berserk over minor problems. He called me up and screamed in my ear and then hung up. He reverted to type, and it began to dawn on me: this guy isn't going to pay me!

Sure enough, Scott fought like the devil over the fee; he lied, and "forgot" things he had agreed to. I ended up with less than half of what I had been promised, and had to file a lawsuit to get part of that.

Could I have avoided this? Could I have seen the real Harry Haight personality behind the friendly mask?

The answer is yes, if I had kept my eyes open and had been honest with myself. (The promise of a large fee helped blind me.)

· First – Scott had a track record of "falling out" with business "friends." His wife even warned me about it.
· Second – Scott *showed* flashes of ruthless and insensitive behavior at unguarded moments.
· Third – I should have gotten a written agreement with Scott early in the game.

Honest people like clear, precise written agreements . . . and they do not object if you ask for one.

Remember that Harry dons a MASK TACTIC when he wants to manipulate, and he does it deliberately. If you are interviewed for a job, you can detect a Harry Haight type of company by certain indications, in spite of a phony front:

· HIGH TURNOVER
· HARRIED, NERVOUS PEOPLE
· AN INAPPROPRIATELY LARGE SALARY OFFER
· A QUICK DECISION TO HIRE YOU (HE COULD FIRE YOU JUST AS FAST)
· TALKING EXCLUSIVELY ABOUT HIMSELF – NOT YOU
· A TARNISHED REPUTATION

THE FRUSTRATION BEHAVIOR OF HARRY HAIGHT

A Frustration Behavior is assumed INVOLUNTARILY. (Remember that the Mask Tactic is *deliberate.*)

The Frustration Behavior *happens* to Harry – it happens when he reaches the point of total frustration. Usually Harry simply gets more aggressive and pushy when he is frustrated. But when he reaches his limit, when he can't take any more, he slips into another role. This is a Frustration Tactic.

When things finally overwhelm Harry, he goes into a Fred Fridgide-type of behavior. He withdraws and says, "To hell with it!" He sulks and feels sorry for himself.

Normally Harry won't stay down too long. But anyone, even the mighty Harry Haight, has a breaking point.

The distinction between a Mask (deliberate and manipulative) and a Frustration Behavior (involuntary) is important. If someone is not "acting" his "normal" role, watch carefully. He is either trying to con you, or he is frustrated beyond endurance.

WHAT BECOMES OF HARRY HAIGHTS?

The real, ingrained Harry Haights of this world...the insatiably power-hungry, ambitious and totally ruthless people...the rare, classic Harry Haights, eventually go down in flames.

History is rich with examples...Nero, Rasputin, Hitler, Mussolini, Napoleon, and many others.* The reason for the eventual destruction of this personality is less divine providence than a basic, intrinsic flaw in the Ruthless/Aggressive makeup.

Eventually the Harry Haight personality goes *too far.* Eventually it crystallizes and becomes rigid against odds which are too formidable. Sooner or later he will roll the dice once too often.

After each disaster, a Harry Haight type of individual will attempt a come back (if he is not destroyed!). Occasionally the agony he creates will cause him to change, to begin to establish mature values. Unfortunately, it is *success* that will often cause Harry's immature personality to surface again. The cycle of disaster/remorse will often plague Harry all his life.

Next we are going to visit another difficult personality, Fred Fridgide. Fred is not uncommon among bosses and employees. He is the dead-ender, the professional victim of life. He got a rotten deal.

---

*For further historical data on the predictable outcome of the Ruthless/Aggressive personality, read: *The Presidential Character: Predicting Performance in the White House* by James David Barber. Particularly fascinating is the section – The Nixon Prediction – an incredibly perceptive forecast written *before* the 1972 elections and Watergate. Prentice-Hall, Inc., Englewood, New Jersey, 1972.

BOSS: HARRY HAIGHT TYPE: RUTHLESS/AGGRESSIVE
VARIATIONS: INTELLECTUAL (Cool, manipulative, clever, sneaky, devastating and deadly)
EMOTIONAL (Loud, coercive, fearless, arrogant, obnoxious, crude and brutal)

GENERAL SKILLS:

LEADERSHIP: A one-man show, motivates largely by fear and by pandering to the greed and baser motives of associates, takes the lion's share of the credit and rewards, short-term leadership sometimes impressive but generates deep resentments and high turnover.

COMMUNICATION: Strictly one-way...not interested in input or other ideas, unless he can secretly acquire them and claim authorship for them, a poor listener who prefers to dominate all conversations.

MOTIVATIONAL ABILITIES: Possesses strictly short-term motivational abilities, employees resent his overbearing attitude and failure to live up to his promises. This also contributes to a constant turnover.

GENERAL PHILOSOPHY:

Shoots from the hip, often hires without careful consideration and on an emotional basis, must usually offer high salaries, dismisses as quickly and thoughtlessly as he hires.

TRAINING: Pays lip service to training but does not use it except as a self-enhancement technique. (Trained people are appendages to do his bidding under strict control).

TEAMWORK: Believes he is too strong to need others, disdains co-operation and mutual trust.

PRODUCT: Make as cheaply as possible, as flashy as possible, advertise and promote as intently as possible. Sell at a lower price, avoid service or long-term commitments.

MAKING DECISIONS: Strictly a loner — all decisions are made relative to Harry's own welfare. If the particular decision can result in an enhancement of his ego or fortunes, it will be so made. Scorns suggestions and assistance, he is too brilliant to need these.

110

CREATIVITY:	A great plagiarist of ideas and concepts, considers real creativity in others as a threat . . . he must put his stamp on everything.
RESEARCH & DEVELOPMENT:	Generally only short-term for immediate results, especially if the results can be used to hurt competitors. Seldom are long-range projects pursued.
PUBLIC RELATIONS:	Considered to be a waste of time, doesn't sell product, a con-job by an agency to make a businessman feel good.
COMPETITION:	*THE ENEMY* . . . give no quarter. It is kill or be killed. Try to run competition right out of business if possible.
DELEGATING:	Seldom delegates authority and power, often delegates responsibility . . . holds real power tightly, wants absolute control.
PEOPLE IN GENERAL:	Not to be trusted, especially employees. Fair game to manipulate, but spy on them or they will pull something. If they don't do as they are told replace them; if they do, burn them out and *then* replace them.

OPERATIVE SKILLS:

SETTING OBJECTIVES:	Announces objectives as if a command, does not consult with employees but rather presents plans as edicts, untouchable sacred cows.
PLANNING STRATEGY:	Considers this area his secret domain, does not respect the opinion of others. He always knows best, is only "foiled" by poor execution of his brilliant ideas.
FOLLOW UP:	Spotty, never consistent. Often assigns and then abandons projects. Follow-up is used as a weapon rather than a nourishing communication.
DEVELOPING A COMPANY PHILOSOPHY:	Usually an elaborate smokescreen for short-term goals . . . seldom adheres to any meaningful continuing policy except in matters of his control . . . often pays lip service to enlightened principles for manipulative purposes.
STANDARDS AND POLICY:	All activities are to be done Harry's way . . . policy is used to enforce his authority. Harry violates policy when expedient, attacks others for any policy violations.

111

AN OVERVIEW OF HARRY HAIGHT...

FREEDOM FACTORS:

• TRIES TO PROVE INDEPENDENCE... ACTUALLY NEEDS OTHER PEOPLE TO BE AROUND HIM TO BULLY AND POSTURE FOR

• UNABLE TO TRANSCEND EVERYDAY LIFE... LACKING IN THE ABILITY TO BE OBJECTIVE

• AN ACTIVE AGENT... A DOER

COGNITION FACTORS:

• SEES THE WORLD AND PEOPLE AS DANGEROUS ...FILTERS OUT POSITIVE DATA...

• EGOISTIC

LOVE FACTORS:

• EGO-CENTERED, MANIPULATIVE RELATIONSHIPS... USUALLY STORMY AND SHORT-LIVED

CREATIVE FACTORS:

• SPONTANEOUS AND UNAFRAID TO ACT

• AN EGO-CENTERED PROBLEM SOLVER – POOR OBJECTIVITY

• SELDOM DEEPLY CREATIVE, A PLAGIARIST WHO ALWAYS CLAIMS CREDIT

INNER-CONNECTION FACTORS:

• USUALLY WEAK...IS EITHER BRUTALLY INTELLECTUAL OR EMOTIONAL, NO DEEP RESERVOIRS OF THOUGHT

HUMANISTIC FACTORS:

• CYNICAL AND COUNTER-VALUING ABOUT OTHER PEOPLE

• NO SELF-HUMOR

• SARDONIC ATTITUDES

• SEES THE WORLD AS DARK AND UNFRIENDLY

• DEEP NEEDS FOR STATUS SYMBOLS

• EXPLOITATIVE OF THE WEAK

• PREJUDICED AND CHAUVINISTIC

*NOTE!
THERE IS NO
"PURE" HARRY
IN REAL LIFE...
YOUR BOSS
MAY BE WELL-
DEVELOPED IN
SOME AREAS,
YET REMAIN
A BASIC RUTHLESS/
AGGRESSIVE INDIVIDUAL!

POINTS TO REMEMBER:

LISTEN ACTIVELY!
SUMMARIZE!
TALK HIM TIRED!
QUESTION!
PROBE!
GET HIM INTO A
PROBLEM-SOLVING MODE!
KNOW YOUR
FACTS!

—NEVER, NEVER let Harry provoke or intimidate you into an argument...never become defensive.

—LISTEN TO HARRY...Listen ACTIVELY and SUMMARIZE his statements.

—WHEN HARRY goes berserk TALK HIM TIRED...and try to move him into a PROBLEM—SOLVING MODE.

—QUESTION and PROBE Harry's flat assertions.

—KNOW YOUR FACTS! Then stick to your guns and hold your ground.

—USE the BOLD PAUSE...the ICEBERG STARE, AND the AUTHORITATIVE ACTIVITY to break the intra-action cycle.

REFERENCES:

Buzzotta, Lefton & Sherberg: <u>EFFECTIVE SELLING THROUGH PSYCHOLOGY: DIMENSIONAL SALES AND SALES MANAGEMENT STRATEGIES</u>, Wiley Interscience, New York, 1972

James Barber: <u>THE PRESIDENTIAL CHARACTER: PREDICTING PERFORMANCE IN THE WHITE HOUSE</u>, Prentice-Hall, Inc., Englewood Cliffs, New Jersey, 1972

John Narcisco and David Burkett: <u>DECLARE YOURSELF, DISCOVERING THE ME IN RELATIONSHIPS</u>, Prentice-Hall, Inc., Englewood Cliffs, New Jersey, 1975

Colin Wilson: <u>THE OUTSIDER</u>, Dell Publishing Co., New York, 1956

Adam V. Vlam: <u>STALIN — THE MAN AND HIS ERA</u>, Viking Press, New York, 1973

John Toland: <u>ADOLF HITLER</u>, Doubleday & Company, New York, 1976

Robert M. Branson, Ph.D.: <u>COPING WITH DIFFICULT PEOPLE</u>, Anchor Press, Doubleday, Garden City, New York, 1981

Robert R. Blake & Jane Srygley Mouton: <u>THE GRID FOR SALES EXCELLENCE</u>, McGraw-Hill, New York, 1980

Robert R. Blake & Jane Srygley Mouton: <u>THE VERSATILE MANAGER</u>, Dow—Jones Irwin, Homewood, Illinois, 1978

Les Donaldson: <u>HOW TO USE PSYCHOLOGICAL LEVERAGE TO DOUBLE THE POWER OF WHAT YOU SAY</u>, Parker Publishing Company, West Nyack, N.Y., 1978

Albert Z. Carr: <u>BUSINESS AS A GAME</u>, Signet, New York, 1969

FRED SEEMS SUSPICIOUS
AND TIMID AT FIRST . . .

YOU ARE ushered into the office of Fred Fridgide. It is a modest, neat and sterile place, with an almost tangible, depressing air.

Fred seems quite suspicious and timid at first, very cool and withdrawn. However, as he senses that you are sincere, and that you are honestly interested in him, he begins to open up and talk.

"The problem with all the motivation theories," Fred says with deep conviction, "is that they simply do not work.

"People will do only that which they want to do. You cannot make them do more, you cannot motivate them!

"Now, I tell you this openly. I am a realistic person. This is a sick, brutal world. The best way to cope with it is to avoid as much trouble, particularly *people* trouble, as possible.

"That's why I never get involved with my employees' jobs – at least no more than absolutely necessary. They will do what they decide they want to do. Problems have a way of solving themselves if you leave them alone long enough.

115

"The leadership of this company was passed on to me by my father. No one asked me if I really wanted it, they just sort of took me for granted.

"But I do my best, and the company has not changed one bit since I've been president.

"Now, I will admit that we've slipped in sales . . . but that is beyond my control. The public is more and more fickle and does not have product loyalty anymore.

"No one manufactures better kerosene lamps than we do.

"Actually, I never wanted to be president of this company anyway. I wanted to play the cello professionally. My dad forced me into this trap . . . why mince words? He ruined my life.

"We don't need any innovators. And − we definitely don't need a lot of headaches by trying to introduce new products.

"So we aren't aggressive. So what! We've survived for 72 years! We don't *want* to be leaders . . . what good is a dead hero?"

Fred slumps in his chair glumly.

"I hate this business! I hate it! I hate the employees! I hate the customers! I hate the suppliers!

"Wait until you meet our idiot cafeteria manager, Nadine Nice. She is so phony with her goody-goody crap . . . she is sickening.

"My son-in-law is different . . . He is actually *dangerous*. He thinks he's tough. He thinks he's able to push me around . . . hell! He won't sit in this chair as long as I'm alive! He'll never get any of his crazy ideas past me either!

"Sometimes though, I just want to say the hell with it and forget it. Let him take over. Why fight it?

"I never had a fair chance in life. I married too young; I got stuck here; I've always been the guy who got the short end.

"All I want is a little peace and quiet and security. If I can keep this company at the same level, that's all I ask.

"Remember one thing. You are talking to a survivor . . . don't you ever forget that. I'm a survivor!

"What am I telling you all of this for? You don't care. Leave me alone!"

Fred buries his nose in some papers, and without another word you leave his office.

6

FRED FRIDGIDE...
The Hostile/Timid
Boss

...How He Rules with Cold Withdrawal and Cynicism...
and How to Insulate Yourself from
His Negative "Drag"

A S YOU leave the office of Fred Fridgide, you are depressed and feel drained. Fred has that effect on people.

Down the hall from Fred is the office of his son-in-law, Dan Deadly. Unlike Fred Fridgide (who is a Hostile/Timid personality type), Dan is a Ruthless/Aggressive individual.

On the door in large gold letters is: "DANIEL B. DEADLY EXECUTIVE VICE-PRESIDENT."

117

"GET A MOVE ON, WILL YOU?"

FRED FRIDGIDE, AS SEEN THROUGH THE EYES OF DAN DEADLY

You enter, and you note the costly fixtures and furniture. The office is much larger and more luxurious than Fred's. Behind a huge oak desk sits Dan. You are about to say hello when he interrupts you.

"Get a move on will you? I've got important stuff to do." You sit down in one of the tiny, uncomfortable chairs near his desk. The back of Dan's chair towers above you both.

"OK...so what do you want to know? Want to know why the company is on the brink of ruin? Huh? Well, it's because of that gutless, cold-natured jerk down the hall!

"Fred has been dead from the neck up for years...he lets everybody run right over him, including me. All he's ever done is sit in that office and feel sorry for himself.

"He's afraid to try *anything* new! Fred's just holding on, and, my friend, that is how you *lose*.

"Fred is more interested in forms and reports than he is in realities...he claims he is really as assertive as anyone else, and the difference is that he has more finesse...that's baloney!

"He's sarcastic and negative. Nothing pleases him. You just can't communicate with him...he won't listen, and he won't talk.

"I know he probably told you that I'm too loud...well, someone has got to push! I make this whole company function. If Fred died and you stuffed him and left him in his office nobody would know the difference...and the tight SOB won't even give me a raise...I have to juggle my expense account to live.

"Fred is so henpecked you wouldn't believe it. He stays here for long hours reading mail and playing president because he hates to go home.

"Actually, he just sort of lets me run things by default. But he won't let me actually TAKE over! He guts my projects, and stuff just sits on his desk. But he won't openly stand up to me. When I take over there'll be some REAL changes made!

"By the way, whatever you do, don't eat in the company cafeteria! It's garbage!

"The cafeteria has lost money for 18 years; everybody hates it, and the first thing I'm gonna do is fire that dodo who runs it, Nadine Nice. That big phony!

"Well, look, how about beating it? I got a hell of a lot of work to do..."

Dan turns his back on you, and you leave without comment.

FRED FRIDGIDE...AS SEEN THROUGH THE EYES OF TIM TEPID

Our next stop is Tim Tepid, the maintenance engineer. His "office" is more like a closet. Tim is a Hostile/Timid Type, just like his boss, Fred Fridgide. Of course, Tim doesn't know this personality similarity exists, and this makes his viewpoint quite interesting.

"Fred? Fred's OK as bosses go. He's as good as any other lucky bastard who inherited a business...

"Me...I've always had to work for a living. Nothing was ever handed to me. I never even got a chance to get educated.

"Anyway, Fred's a lot better than his crazy son-in-law. I hope that maniac never gets control of the company.

"I GET EVEN THOUGH.."

"Things are pretty bad around here...they just seem to get worse and worse.

"I should have been given a raise four years ago...but try to get a decent raise around here!

"But, I don't say nothin'. Old Tim doesn't stick his neck out!

"And I ain't quittin' either! Not me. Just get into some worse situation."

Tim lowers his voice and looks around.

"I get even though...between you and me. They sent an order down the other day with the wrong part number on it. Hell, I knew it, but I went ahead and ordered 35 of 'em! Ha! That caused 'em plenty of trouble!

"You better believe I saved a copy of the original order to stick under their nose! Tim Tepid knows how to look after himself.

"Yeah, I know I ain't getting nowhere. So what? If you don't get the breaks, you don't get the breaks. I just hang in – and they ain't never been able to get anything on me.

"I do all my reports, and all my work...nothin' extra, you know, 'cause that would just draw attention to me.

"I just hope Fred leaves me alone. And, *that* he does. I ain't seen him in eight months. He just hides up there in his office.

"Which is good.

"Who needs him?"

FRED FRIDGIDE ... AS SEEN THROUGH THE EYES OF NADINE NICE

After a horrible free meal in the company cafeteria, you meet Nadine Nice, the Warm/Timid manager. Nadine smiles broadly and offers you her hand.

"Well! Well! Hope you enjoyed that hearty meal!" Nadine says.

"Haven't you just loved touring our company? Real teamwork, eh? Sure we have our problems, but you met quite a group of fellows, didn't you?

"I'll bet you enjoyed talking to Mr. Fridgide—nice man, a very hard-working individual. Just a bit on the shy and modest side.

"I try to cheer him up whenever I can. Fred has so many responsibilities; his job is *so* hard on him.

"Of course, it would help *me* if Fred gave me some encouragement. You know, a nod or a pat on the back once in a while. But – gosh – he is so burdened!

"You know, Mr. Fridgide is really a warm person underneath it all! He just needs to relax and take it easy now and then... you know, let his hair down a bit.

"One thing sure, this company will never change as long as Mr. Fridgide is in charge ... and I like that. It makes me feel secure.

"FRED DIDN'T SPEAK TO ME
FOR FIVE YEARS AFTER THE INCIDENT ..."

"I admit I was a little discouraged when only 3 other people showed up at the company picnic I planned ... a lot of food went to waste. But, it was cloudy that day.

"Folks need to get together and learn to like each other. That's all this world needs. And that's my strong point, I build many meaningful relationships.

"I guess that's why I'm so liked by Mr. Fridgide ... although he did get really angry at me once. Wow! That was the time the health department closed us down ... the cafeteria failed inspection and we were fined.

"I explained to Mr. Fridgide that the health department people were just doing their job, and that the problem was really my fault. I think Fred admired my courage in taking the responsibility, and he didn't fire me ... although he didn't speak to me for five years after the incident. That bothered me.

"I know folks like to kid about the food here, but deep down they really like me and know I sincerely try.

"Say, how would you like to see some pictures of my family?"

FRED FRIDGIDE AS SEEN THROUGH THE EYES OF STAN STABLE

Stan Stable, the Compassionate/Assertive Customer Service Manager, greets you warmly. After exchanging a few preliminary remarks, Stan comes right to the point.

"To be frank," Stan says, "Fred is a difficult man to work for.

"He sets no objectives, does no real planning. He just goes through the motions of managing ...

"Fred's heart just isn't in it ... The company has fallen behind the times. We maintain a decent customer service record, but our products do not come up to competitive standards.

"Even so, Fred will not address this problem ... 'What will be, will be' is his philosophy. In fact, Fred's attitude about all problems is the same: ignore them and they will go away.

"I work hard to win Fred's confidence, and I guess he trusts me much more than anyone else.

"FRED'S HEART JUST ISN'T IN IT . . ."

"It takes great effort to get Fred to agree to any kind of a constructive action plan. Fred kind of makes a career out of being a victim of 'circumstances beyond his control.'

"Consequently, our company lacks initiative. We have no – I mean *no* program for product development. Fred is simply a kind of bridge to the past, he functions to pass on the original ideas of his father. These ideas are simply not appropriate to the current situation.

"Fred cannot, or really will not officially delegate anything. He does not seem to believe in cultivating personnel or in trusting his staff.

"There is no team spirit, no growth, and there is poor morale.

"Naturally I'm discouraged by the oppressive atmosphere here. I wish I could say something positive about Fred, but I cannot.

"Please understand that I do not blame Fred and the company for slowing my personal growth. The time here has been a growing experience. Even though I recognize this as a difficult situation, the responsibility for my life is my own.

"In my judgment this company shows clearly the results of what happens when all decisions are safety decisions, and never growth decisions.

"Personally, I will make an appropriate growth decision for my career when the time comes."

FRED ONLY WANTS TO SURVIVE

THE REAL FRED FRIDGIDE

Fred Fridgide is indeed a man afraid.

He sees the world much as Harry Haight sees it. Fred would agree with Harry that people are dangerous and self-seeking. He is as hostile toward the world around him as Harry Haight is to his world.

But Fred has a very negative self-image. He is not assertive and courageous the way Harry is. He is, in fact, timid.

He seeks order, security, predictability, sameness.

Yet, even though Fred is timid, he is not helpless. His passiveness is obvious, but he bitterly resents anyone who takes advantage of him.

Fred broods and plans revenge against anyone who would exploit him.

Fred is a dead-ender, the original loser.

You could contrast Fred's situation with Harry's in this manner:

Harry Haight is a man on a log roll, running faster and faster to keep from falling...while Fred is holding on to his log and trying to keep it from moving!

Each man sees the "waters" around him as dangerous and "shark" infested, yet each takes a different attitude...Harry is a fighter and he refuses to show any fear; Fred is a "hanger-on" who only wants to survive.

SIX POSITIVE TACTICS FOR HANDLING FRED FRIDGIDE

You are dealing with a man who is suspicious, and who needs reassurance. Dealing with Fred requires great patience.

Fred will attempt to handle problems by indirectly rejecting them. He avoids them, rather than directly challenging them. Fred avoids by procrastinating, by refusing to comment upon a situation, by simply withdrawing and acting indifferent, and by making one objection after another to suggested solutions.

TACTIC #1: PROJECT A REASSURING, DEPENDABLE IMAGE

– Slow down! You need to move almost in slow motion or you will cause Fred to withdraw.

– Dress conservatively, don't project a flashy, tasteless image.

– Be moderate in your speech . . . pitch your voice a tone or two lower and modulate it pleasantly.

– Never act familiar, or too quickly assume Fred has been won over. Do not take Fred's trust for granted; you must rebuild this relationship virtually every day.

– Fred hates aggressive people, but he also has a deep distrust of a sugary, goody-goody individual.

– Use short sentences and moderate words, never try to impress him with large words and complicated thinking.

– Project candor and honesty.

– Know your subject, be confident and pleasant.

TACTIC #2: QUESTION! LISTEN! CONSIDER!

One of the better ways to break the ice with Fred is to use probing questions and masterful *pauses*.

– When you ask a question, wait patiently for the answer. Sooner or later Fred will speak, and when he does, *consider his words carefully.*

– When Fred does reply, wait for a bit before you answer or make another statement; Fred will distrust you if you too quickly shoot from the hip and reply instantly.

TACTIC #3: PAUSE! PAUSE! PAUSE!

– The pause is the most effective weapon in your arsenal for dealing with Fred Fridgide. NEVER talk to fill up the spaces and the gaps in the conversation. These gaps are the parts of a communication situation that Fred likes best!

– If Fred begins a particular behavior to avoid listening to you, like looking out of a window or reading something, simply pause. Wait until he is tracking you again.

– Remember that Fred does not perform these actions of avoidance to be consciously rude and insensitive. They are simply habits he has developed. They are not directed toward you, but rather at life in general.

– Deep down Fred wants to be led – but he does not want to be taken advantage of. Leading Fred along without seeming to dominate him requires unusual skill.

– Do not be disturbed if pauses last several minutes. Wait Fred out. Understanding the power of a pause can greatly improve your skills as a communicator.

Once I was attempting to sell an expensive advertising program to two cautious, tough men. One was president of the company and the other was the general manager.

I had just been cautioned by a master salesman that I tended to talk too much in a presentation. He said, "After you make your presentation and ask for the sale, SHUT UP."

After a long and careful demonstration, I said: "It will take a couple of weeks to get the program ready after you accept it. When do you want me to get into production?"

(This is known as "asking for the sale.")

Eight minutes went by without a *single word* from either man. I was ready to burst – but I was determined not to speak first. Finally the president spoke. "OK," he said, "you can start producing it immediately." And that was that.

Pauses serve as a valuable respite for people to consider what you have said; they provide a reassuring rest from the stress of active communication.

TACTIC #4: LEAD — TAKE THE INITIATIVE — BUT NEVER, NEVER PUSH!

– Fred wants you to make decisions for him . . . but he never wants to be pushed . . . you must guide him to obvious conclusions and then leave him alone.

– Fred will permit you a degree of latitude if he believes that he can trust you, and that you are dependable and honest.

TACTIC #5: TRY TO GET FRED INVOLVED

This can be accomplished by the process of probing, by asking for his advice and *listening carefully.*

– Never be phony with Fred (or anyone else!), but seek to compliment him if you can honestly do so . . . seek to establish some common ground for better communication. (In Fred Fridgide's case, some knowledge of the cello would be very helpful!)

TACTIC #6: KNOW THE FACTS! BUT DON'T OVERWHELM FRED!

– Fred hates someone who lords over him; he can't stand an aggressive pusher like Dan Deadly. On the other hand Fred is impressed by someone who has confidence, who knows his subject and can communicate it.

– Use reassuring communication, but never act ingratiating. Fred is often an emotional drag, so try to get "up" for your conversations with him and never let him know he is annoying you or draining your enthusiasm.

THE MASK TACTICS OF FRED FRIDGIDE

Little need be said about the mask tactics and strategies of Fred Fridgide. Fred almost never uses a mask of any kind. He simply cannot stomach acting the part of Gary Goodman . . . and he cannot sustain the part of Mike Mature.

Once in a while Fred will come on like Harry Haight, but this is a rare situation.

The reason Fred doesn't often attempt to use mask tactics is that he believes people will do what they want to in the end anyway, and they cannot be influenced. So why go through all the work of a mask strategy?

Even when Fred does attempt to use a mask, he does so without conviction and is very lackluster about it. He seems to sense his attempt to influence another is doomed to failure, so why try?

When seriously frustrated, Fred acts *more* and *more* like Fred – more withdrawn, more hostile, more self-pitying. Occasionally he can be driven to the breaking point, and he will involuntarily fall into a frustration behavior. He begins to act like Harry Haight.

This Harry Haight role doesn't last long, and Fred continues to seethe long after the situation that set him off has been resolved. Fred never, never apologizes for acting like Harry.

WHAT WILL BECOME OF FRED FRIDGIDE?

Fred makes a career out of being a martyr: a victim.

He never sees his situation as his own fault. It was created by circumstances beyond his control.

Therefore, Fred is not responsible. He cannot be responsible for himself and his failings if he is a "victim!" There are multitudes of people who use this technique of avoiding responsibility for themselves.

Choosing to be a "victim" establishes all problems as outside of oneself, and no one can blame an innocent bystander. On the other hand, this attitude also grants the power of control to forces on the outside; it abdicates responsibility.

Fred's passive, fearful, negative and unplanned attitude toward life leads to a pointless, meaningless, dreary and unfocused existence.

Fred Fridgides are self-pitying dead-enders; they collect thousands of imaginary "martyr medals," and suffer in silence.

Fred would never stand up and say: "My condition is my fault! My unhappiness is my fault! My discontent is my fault!"

And so, Fred Fridgides drift through life like psychic "vampires," draining the positive forces and energies away from all who come in contact with them. When "Freds" finally pass from the active business scene they are not missed. They continue to live a hollow bitter existence, as long as they continue to "survive."

Fred lost his heart, his desire, his courage and initiative long ago. For whatever reason, he has given up.

There is a little Fred Fridgide in all of us – especially when we become discouraged or lose our initiative. We pull out of such moods. With Fred, this is a way of life that rarely changes.

· · · · · ·

Next, let us visit one more immature boss, the incredible Gary Goodman. Don't sell him short – Gary can be as dangerous and trying as any other immature boss, if you let him.

BOSS: FRED FRIDGIDE   TYPE: HOSTILE/TIMID
VARIATIONS: CHRONIC (Ingrained, habitual responses)
              SITUATIONAL (Frustration Behavior caused
              by inability to handle stress situation)

GENERAL SKILLS:

LEADERSHIP:
Very poor ... prefers to delay action — avoids all problems ... Relies on over-administered policy system to keep things running.

COMMUNICATION:
No-Way Communicator ... neither tries to give nor to receive information.

MOTIVATIONAL ABILITIES:
Non-existent ... has no faith in motivational programs because "people just do what they want to do anyway."

GENERAL PHILOSOPHY:

Sees world as a hostile, dangerous place and feels inadequate to cope with it ... distrusts everyone.

TRAINING:
Of no value ... people are not willing to learn anyway. On the other hand, believes in strictly structuring personnel into slots.

TEAMWORK:
Fred wants no part of being on a team or being a team leader. Teams are dangerous and difficult to control. Keep personnel fragmented and isolated.

PRODUCT:
Make it good enough to get by; market share is not affected by product quality unless it is so bad that it causes a negative reaction.

MAKING DECISIONS:
Avoids decisions, puts them off when possible. When he must choose, he always chooses "safety decisions" over "growth decisions."

CREATIVITY:
Fred is personally not creative, prefers the status quo. Distrusts creativity in others; atmosphere of company is negative and destructive to innovative ideas.

RESEARCH & DEVELOPMENT:
Not necessary.

PUBLIC RELATIONS:	Public will think whatever it wants to think, you cannot influence this.
COMPETITION:	Avoid direct conflicts, take what is left.
DELEGATING:	Does not delegate authority, only responsibility. Motto: "It is not whether you win or lose, but how you place the blame."
PEOPLE IN GENERAL:	Untrustworthy, deceitful, lazy . . . and they do only what they want to do for their own selfish reasons . . . people never change.

OPERATIVE SKILLS:

SETTING OBJECTIVES:	No long-range objectives . . . main objective is to avoid problems, survive, and to preserve the status quo.
PLANNING STRATEGY:	No long-range strategies . . . very stilted and conservative tactics.
FOLLOW UP:	Spotty . . . seldom amounts to more than negative complaints about production or execution.
DEVELOPING A COMPANY PHILOSOPHY:	Rarely more than a determination to survive at all costs . . . not subject to revision.
STANDARDS AND POLICY:	Stick to the existing rules . . . don't rock the boat.

131

AN OVERVIEW OF FRED FRIDGIDE...

FREEDOM FACTORS:

- WEAK AND DEPENDENT, THOUGH USUALLY A LONER
- A STRICT CONFORMIST
- A NON-ACTIVE AGENT... PASSIVE

COGNITION FACTORS:

- SEES THE WORLD AND PEOPLE IN IT AS DANGEROUS
- FILTERS OUT POSITIVE DATA

CREATIVE FACTORS:

- VIRTUALLY NON-CREATIVE, STIFF AND CONTROLLED

INNER-CONNECTION FACTORS:

- USUALLY A SHALLOW AND NEGATIVE THINKER

LOVE FACTORS:

- USUALLY UNHAPPY, NEGATIVE RELATIONSHIPS

HUMANISTIC FACTORS:

- VIEWS HUMANITY WITH SCORN AND DISLIKE
- NEGATIVE, PESSIMISTIC OUTLOOK
- UNABLE TO LAUGH AT SELF
- PREJUDICED, NEGATIVE AND NARROW PHILOSOPHY

POINTS TO REMEMBER:

— DON'T BE too pushy . . . Fred wants SECURITY, PREDICTABILITY, SAMENESS. Avoid being flashy and aggressive.

— SLOW DOWN . . . Listen ACTIVELY to Fred . . . QUESTION and PROBE and be patient while he ponders your statements . . . QUESTION! LISTEN! LISTEN!

— PAUSE: Using pauses pays great dividends . . . Fred loves them more than communication . . . The PAUSE is your most potent weapon . . . MASTER IT!

— SPEAK SOFTLY and KNOW YOUR SUBJECT!

— BE WILLING to take the initiative but NEVER PUSH or take advantage of Fred's passive attitude.

— TAKE YOUR TIME and develop a situation of TRUST.

133

REFERENCES:

Bussota, Lefton & Sherberg: <u>EFFECTIVE SELLING THROUGH PSYCHOLOGY: DIMENSIONAL SALES AND SALES MANAGEMENT STRATEGIES</u>, Wiley Interscience, New York, 1972

James Barber: <u>THE PRESIDENTIAL CHARACTER: PREDICTING PERFORMANCE IN THE WHITE HOUSE</u>, Prentice-Hall, Inc., Englewood Cliffs, New Jersey, 1972

Les Donaldson: <u>HOW TO USE PSYCHOLOGICAL LEVERAGE TO DOUBLE THE POWER OF WHAT YOU SAY</u>, Parker Publishing Company, Inc., West Nyack, New York, 1978

Robert R. Blake & Jane Srygley Mouton: <u>THE GRID FOR SUPERVISORY EFFECTIVENESS</u>, Scientific Methods, Inc., Austin, Texas, 1975

Robert M. Bramson, Ph.D.: <u>COPING WITH DIFFICULT PEOPLE</u>, Anchor Press, Doubleday, Garden City, New York, 1981

W. Hugh Missildine: <u>YOUR INNER CHILD OF THE PAST</u>, Simon and Schuster, New York, 1963

T.A. Harris: <u>I'M OK — YOU'RE OK</u>, Avon Books, New York, 1969

Dr. Donald W. Cole: <u>PROFESSIONAL SUICIDE, A SURVIVAL KIT FOR YOU AND YOUR JOB</u>, McGraw-Hill, New York, 1981

SHE TOSSES SOME PAPERS ON GARY'S DESK.

"WELCOME!... welcome," says Gary Goodman as you enter his traditionally furnished office.

You notice that another man is in the office, evidently having coffee with Gary.

"Excuse me," you say. "I didn't realize that you were busy."

"Oh, come on in and sit down!" Gary smiles. "I've no secrets from Lorn. Shake hands with my public relations expert, Lorn Love."

You introduce yourself to the pleasant-looking man and shake his hand. He beams warmly at you.

"Lorn and I spend a couple of hours each day reviewing things ...public relations matters and various personnel situations. We are what you might call 'people experts.'"

Gary continues exuberantly: "I'm so proud of the Goodman Biscuit Company! As you will discover, we are all one big happy family...you simply will not find any problems, that is, *people problems* in this company."

Suddenly Gary's door bangs open. A thin, sullen, frowning woman of about 45 stalks in. She tosses some papers on Gary's desk.

"Oh! Cindy," Gary forces a smile, seemingly somewhat embarrassed. "I would like you to meet someone..." Gary nods in your direction.

"Hello." Cindy says coldly. She then turns and walks out.

"Well, excuse Cindy, please," says Gary. "She works so hard and worries so much.

"It distresses me to see Cindy upset. I must have done something to offend her. Well...I'll talk to her later.

"Now, as you tour our factory you will notice an absence of competition. Isn't that right, Lorn?"

"Oh yes!" says Lorn. "Our employees are not subjected to competitive situations. We don't believe in 'competition.'"

"Yes!" Gary agrees. "And our customers love us! We have one of the most liberal policies for returns and refunds in the industry...in fact, this policy costs us plenty.

"But we have an abundance of friends out there, and that's what counts. Being nice pays off.

"Oh, we may have a problem now and then...just as any family would. Ha! My motto is: 'Ignore problems to death!'

"Forgive me for adding one other point. Employee motivation is simply a myth. People do just as they want to do.

"Keep 'em happy – make employees your friends – and you'll succeed.

"That's why Lorn and I were so shocked about the strike last year. Gosh, we were amazed that some folks were not pleased with us...right Lorn?"

"Yes, sir!" says Lorn. "And we were really hurt when they burned down the northside plant...even though it was a rather old plant.

"I must say," Lorn continued, "that our company is reunited and happy again. You can just *feel* it.

"And the man behind it all is right there, Gary Goodman!"

"Oh Lorn," Gary gushes, "it's men like you who made the difference."

"No Gary," says Lorn, "it was you! You are the man we depend on. It is you who kept our quality up and kept our package the same as it was when we were founded 63 years ago. It's you who won the hearts of employees...

"Gary is more than a boss, I tell you. He is a friend, a man of genuine warmth, one of the most generous men I know. Gary is a 'people' person.

"Gary and I often spend mornings exchanging ideas for hours. Not many bosses would take the time to do that.

"But Gary isn't appreciated the way he should be."

"Well, thanks, Lorn," Gary blushes. "Lorn and I are a team, that's for sure. And so is the entire company. Lorn and I handle the people situations; Ted Tiger is a fighter and a driver; Cindy is expert at paper work and regulations; Barbara Bright is an all-round performer. What a team!

"I guess that's the Goodman Biscuit story...we aren't fancy by some standards. No expensive agencies, no costly market studies. Our sales people are our best source of information, not cold statistics.

"Have a nice look around. Enjoy yourself!"

7

GARY GOODMAN ...
The Warm/Timid
Boss

... How He Rules with Manipulative
"Goody-Goody" Tactics, and How to Handle Him
without Creating Friction

A FTER LEAVING Gary's office you feel a comfortable glow, but also a vague apprehension about something you perceive as lacking in Gary's attitude.

Gary is easy-going, relaxed and warm, as is his friend Lorn Love.

But you had difficulty pinning Gary down to specifics; the conversation (presented in much condensed form here) rambled around without focus or purpose.

Neither Gary nor Lorn seemed concerned about business. They seemed to be willing to let things slide as they discussed rather trivial matters.

You head down the hall to the office of Ted Tiger.

"GARY, WHAT THE HELL ARE YOU TRYING TO DO TO ME . . . ?"

GARY GOODMAN AS SEEN THROUGH THE EYES OF TED TIGER, THE RUTHLESS/AGGRESSIVE SALES MANAGER

Ted is the National Sales Manager for the Goodman Biscuit Company. After his secretary lets you into his office, Ted ignores you for some time. He is engrossed in some papers he is reading.

Suddenly Ted throws the papers down.

"That idiot!" Ted exclaims. "He wants to give away the store!

"Can you believe Gary accepted the return of 30 cases of Gooey Goodies from a dealer who claims my man 'high pressured' him into buying?

"Gary will break this company some day! Now! What do you want, anyway? Oh, I remember, an interview.

"You know, I just don't have time for an interview. Can't you see who really runs this company? No wonder I'm so busy!

"Let me show you something."

Ted dials an extension on his telephone and Gary Goodman answers plainly over the desk speaker, "This is Mr. Goodman."

"Gary . . . what in the hell are you doing to me?" growls Ted.

"Why Ted — what is the trouble?"

"Gary, you took back those Gooey Goodies from that deadbeat Tyler. He was tricked into buying those cookies fair and square."

"Well, Ted, it seemed like the right thing to do to keep him happy."

"What about keeping *me* happy? And my men happy? Victor Vile is one of my best salesmen...I taught him all he knows."

"I'm sorry Ted. I know you work hard...please relax."

"How can I relax, Gary? You take stuff back faster than I can sell it!"

"Please Ted...I'll pay Victor and you your commissions and bonuses on the sale since you feel as you do...You know I always try to be fair."

"OK Gary...I'll tell Victor."

Ted pushed a button and abruptly cuts off the speaker phone.

"See what I mean? The guy is a pussy cat!

"Him and Lorn have a love-in everyday, a mutual admiration society. They waste time swilling coffee and visiting. The light-weights!

"Gary spends too much time glad-handing and politicking. He vacillates and tries to please everyone. That phony. When the heat really gets on, Gary gets sick, you can count on it.

"What this company needs is some powerhouse advertising and some gut-level selling effort. We need to cut some of the quality out of the products so we can have the dough to promote. People don't appreciate quality anyway.

"We need a flashy, modern package and the best shelf location possible. We need to layoff some of those old workers who can barely walk, and those arrogant new ones who formed a union last year.

"We need – "

The phone suddenly interrupts Ted. Ted answers it with his desk speaker phone.

"Yeah?"

"Ted, this is Mr. Goodman. Ted, I'm a bit concerned about our last conversation. You weren't airing our dirty linen in front of our visitor, were you?"

"Gary! How could you accuse me of that?" Ted winks at you. "I've always been a loyal employee."

"Forgive me Ted...you know I have the highest respect for you..."

"Sure, Gary, forget it." Ted smirks and cuts off the phone.

"See what a little sweet talk does to the idiot?" Ted leans back and lights up a foul-smelling cigar. "Well, I've got a lot of things to do so I'll have to cut this a little short."

· · · · · ·

You now have a far different picture of the Goodman Company. As you leave Ted's office, you realize that the "good will" is only surface and cosmetic.

Gary has problems, but he seems to simply deny and ignore them.

You decide that there is no reason to visit Lorn Love, who is still chatting with Gary anyway, oblivious to his appointment with you. Instead, you make your way to the office of Cindy Chill, the Hostile/Timid Personnel Director.

GARY GOODMAN AS SEEN THROUGH THE EYES OF CINDY CHILL

From your first meeting with Cindy in Gary's office, you sense a withdrawn coolness in Cindy. You get the same feeling when you meet her again.

"I simply do not have much time to talk." Cindy eyes you with suspicion.

"See this report? Gary does such a poor job of filling it out that it takes me hours to unravel it. I can barely read it!

"Gary will not fill out his forms properly. Nor will Lorn or Ted.

"Gary is terrible at detail . . . almost as bad as Ted Tiger.

"And Ted pushes Gary around so much it makes me sick.

"Gary and Lorn spend most of the day telling war stories and drinking coffee . . . and Lorn is overpaid. He is as lazy and worthless a manager as you'll ever see.

"If Gary would just leave me alone. But no! He comes down here regularly to talk to me . . . to tell me how good I am and how much he appreciates me. Baloney!

"Gary just wastes my time. He is a phony, and is not even honest with himself. This is a bitter, cruel world, and Gary goes around as though he doesn't see all the bad surrounding him.

"We had a brutal strike last winter and thousands of dollars worth of equipment was destroyed . . . Gary would not even prosecute!

"Frankly, this is a terrible place to work. I'd leave, but I don't have anywhere to go. I'm too old...it's too late for me.

"I'm just waiting around to die, like everybody else..."

You are drained when you leave the office of Cindy Chill, and are happy to get away from the depressing vibes that seem to surround her.

Your final visit in the Goodman Company is with Barbara Bright, the Home Economist of the organization.

GARY GOODMAN, AS SEEN
THROUGH THE EYES OF
BARBARA BRIGHT,
A COMPASSIONATE/ASSERTIVE EMPLOYEE

The first thing you notice is a remarkable change in atmosphere when you enter the Home Economics Department of the Goodman Biscuit Company. It is more than the pleasant smell of cooking bakery products, there is a relaxed attitude, and yet a dynamic, moving creative spirit in the air.

Barbara is a frank and honest person, and she talks with a twinkle of humor in her eye.

"Gary has some laudable characteristics – he is a sensitive and honest man.

"Gary has seriously tried to maintain the quality of our products, although he is very reluctant about doing new things.

"Gary is stable, almost hidebound in tradition.

"I must say that Gary is somewhat lacking in direction, in focus. He lives in the past, he tends to be non-assertive, even timid.

"Because of what, in my judgment, is a lack of resolution and a tendency to drift, Ted Tiger tends to dominate Gary. Ted manages to get away with murder.

"And, when Ted finally goes too far, he goes into his 'good guy' routine, and Gary finds this irresistible. He falls for it every time.

"Another serious weakness, in my opinion, is that Gary tends to avoid critical problems. He spends much of the day with Lorn Love and the morale of the company suffers greatly due to this.

"For my own part, I try to make my department the finest of its kind. Gary does permit me *latitude* to do this, if not the *budget*.

"Yes, Gary is a gentleman . . . almost too nice for his own good. He reminds me of the poem about the man 'too gentle to live among the wolves . . . '"

THE REAL GARY GOODMAN . . . A MAN ADDICTED TO WARMTH

Gary is a man addicted to the approval of others. He has strong security and esteem needs, and the role of leadership is not comfortable for him.

Gary's addictions color and influence his business behavior, even to the point of hurting his business judgments.

The hunger for warmth that Gary feels is real . . . and a very powerful drive. When Gary is subjected to disapproval or rejection, it can cause him to be depressed and self-pitying for days (an involuntary, Fred Fridgide-type of frustration behavior).

Gary's basic technique is to win approval by being "nice." He bestows warmth and expects warmth in return. Gary seeks to get his way by manipulating, by killing with kindness.

When Gary is thwarted and slips into a sulking mood, he is actually attempting (in some measure) to "get his way" by making others feel guilty.

Meanwhile, critical problems are being ignored . . . because Gary cannot cope with conflict and negative situations.

He tries to mollify and pacify the assertive people around him.

But do not underestimate Gary. Like most Warm/Timid indivi duals, Gary has his own ways of fighting back and getting even. He dislikes and resents being taken advantage of.

Even though Ted seems to dominate Gary, in the crunch Gary gets his own way. And his resentment against Ted will possibly explode someday.

A Ruthless/Aggressive personality like Ted's will eventually cause him to overplay his hand. Count on it.

All in all, Gary is happy with his life. He seldom complains. All the same, he causes others distress because of his inattention to detail and routine.

Gary covers these weaknesses by saying he likes the "people" aspects of his job, and dislikes the fussy "details."

FIVE POSITIVE TACTICS FOR HANDLING GARY GOODMAN

Gary has the power to help, or hurt, your own career.

Precisely because he lacks the skills to achieve, he will eventually find himself in crises.

At these times he will do anything to save himself. He will even hurt you if it is necessary. And, his lack of focus can cause you to lose your own personal motivation, and you could begin to drift.

Many people who work for Gary lose their own desire to achieve, because Gary does not really value achievement as much as he does social graces.

Don't look to Gary for goals and incentives.

TACTIC #1: PROBE INTO GARY'S QUICK AND EASY AGREEMENTS

Because Gary avoids controversy and likes to please, he often misleads people into thinking that he is in agreement with them, when indeed he is not.

Gary will assure you that he understands when he does not, and seem to agree with a course of action when he has no conviction about it at all.

Gary doesn't like to deny anyone anything, so he tends to lead people on. He promises raises when he can't deliver; he holds out hope for promotion when there is no prospect of promotion at all.

"We'll see," is a favorite stall of Gary's.

Be cautious with Gary. He will pull the rug out when you least expect it.

So be sure to pin him down. Resolutely seek to make him take a position that is clear. Ask questions until he is committed. You may cause some hidden objections to emerge, but this is good.

Better to find out what Gary thinks now, before you are out on a limb by yourself.

TACTIC #2: AVOID (YES, AVOID) THE FACTS!

Amazingly, when Gary is presented with detail and supporting data about something, he loses interest.

Gary wants to know that a proposition is sound; he wants to trust you. He wants to believe in you, to have confidence in you.

Unless you are "far-out" as an individual, he will seek to rely on your judgment and avoid the discomfort of making a decision.

Don't overwhelm him with detail; simply give him an outline and offer your conclusions. Give Gary the broad aspects and forget the detailed options.

But – BE RIGHT. You need to live up to the faith that Gary places in you, so base your own decisions on considered data. Be aware of the responsibilities that Gary's immaturity may cause to be diverted to you.

TACTIC #3: DON'T ATTEMPT EXPLOITIVE TACTICS

If Gary gets the idea that you are exploiting his immaturities and his passiveness, he will deeply resent it.

So don't even permit yourself to think in a manipulative manner. Be sincere, and understand that Gary has a fine quality (that of sensitiveness) and that this quality extends to consideration of *your* feelings. Be considerate of *his*.

Warm/Timid Bosses can be good people to work for; they give you scope and an opportunity to assume responsibility. Of course, you must keep in mind that you are generally on your own, and Gary will not likely back you up in a clutch situation.

Under Gary you can gain in self-reliance. You can even guide Gary to an extent, if you happen to be an assertive, strong person.

A passive boss gives an assertive person the opportunity for considerable influence. An individual, who is mature and sensitive in addition to being aggressive, will avoid the temptations of being manipulative and will do very well while working for Gary.

TACTIC #4: LET GARY HAVE HIS ROPE

Gary is not a business-like person. He likes to discuss all manner of things and he avoids tough issues.

Be patient about this. Be firm and strong and re-focus the conversation upon significant matters, but don't be severe and austere.

Permit Gary to re-establish his confidence in your reliability; let him visit with you for awhile. After you have established favorable circumstances for communication, then go on with your business discussion.

TACTIC #5: RECOGNIZE GARY'S NEEDS

Gary is constantly trying to prove his worthiness to enjoy esteem and approval. No matter how many times he achieves this proof, he must renew it over and over again.

Gary seeks to GET warmth by giving it. He also seeks stability, strength and trustworthiness in other people.

Moody, withdrawn people like Cindy Chill disturb Gary. Ruthless/Aggressive people like Ted Tiger cause him great anguish. Gary is most comfortable with the Warm/Timid individual like Lorn Love.

But Gary does recognize ability and confidence, and he will rely on an honest, optimistic and capable employee.

In summary, be considerate and seek initiatives to *do* things for your own maximum self-development under Gary.

THE MASKS OF GARY GOODMAN

Gary rarely uses deliberate mask tactics.

He seldom recognizes or admits hostility in others, and seldom reacts to it. If he encounters undeniable aggression, Gary will become even more Warm/Timid in an effort to placate the individual.

Gary tends to excuse and accept even blatantly immature behavior. He rationalizes other people's actions, and he blames himself for many problems. "It will all work out OK," says Gary, even in the face of impending disaster.

GARY WILL, HOWEVER, SOMETIMES BE PUSHED INTO AN INVOLUNTARY FRUSTRATION-BEHAVIOR PATTERN (NOT A MASK BEHAVIOR).

Even Gary has his breaking point. Usually, when confronted with nasty and unreasonable behavior, Gary will simply intensify his warmth. If this fails, he will probably slip into his frustration behavior.

When this happens Gary might even erupt like Harry Haight, although this will be a short-lived tirade and be deeply regretted later.

Even when Gary's anger is justified, he may apologize for it. This leaves him wide open for guilt-manipulation.

Gary might also, under extreme pressure, slip into a behavior that resembles Fred Fridgide – withdrawing in self-pity.

Even this withdrawal is calculated, although not consciously. It is an attempt to manipulate or influence someone else's behavior (as Harry Haight's temper tantrums are). Gary is saying (in effect), "I am hurt, and I am such a nice person. You should feel guilty. I will keep being hurt until you move to help me or begin to act as I wish you to act."

WHAT WILL BECOME OF GARY GOODMAN?

It is likely that Gary will go along in his benign manner, not making waves, not causing trouble, and continuing to deny problems.

His company will suffer, of course. But to his credit, Gary maintains a quality product and tries to be fair with his customers.

On the other hand, because his company lacks dynamics and a realistic attitude toward competition, it is vulnerable.

There was a typically Ruthless/Aggressive company that marketed appliances on a mass national scale several years ago. This company brutally bulldozed competition, advertised voluminously, slashed prices and tried to destroy established businesses. It began to quickly move into, and dominate, one large market after another.

In one good-sized midwestern city, this driving company opened a store with a massive grand-opening campaign. Amazingly, the leading appliance dealer in this city (a Warm/Timid company with 60 years of tradition) ran a full page ad welcoming the new company to the city.

Cynically, the Ruthless/Aggressive organization began slashing prices and undercutting the local store. Within two years the traditional old store that had welcomed competition was completely out of business.

The point is: even the laudable qualities of sensitivity and warmth need to be augmented by assertiveness and practicality, or they will simply be swept aside.

Unfortunately, people like Gary, when they are frustrated, often attempt to desensitize themselves rather than simply asserting themselves.

It is possible, although it is a rare combination, to be both assertive *and* sensitive.

In fact, Mike Mature has both of these qualities.

• • • • • •

In our final visit we go to a company that is mature and wholesome, a company that nourishes its employees instead of exploiting and destroying them.

This is the company of Mike Mature.

BOSS: GARY GOODMAN **TYPE: WARM/TIMID**

VARIATIONS: HEARTY, BACKSLAPPING (Loud, outgoing extroverted)

BENIGN (Mr. Goodguy, never-ask-for-what-you-want, manipulates through guilt stimulation)

GENERAL SKILLS:

LEADERSHIP:

Gary is more of a companion and friend than a leader...avoids the limelight, ducks difficult issues, controversy puts him into panic.

COMMUNICATION:

A partial 2-way communicator, although Gary will listen he tends to gloss over difficulties and agrees too quickly with things he has reservations about, screens out negatives.

MOTIVATIONAL ABILITIES:

Tries to motivate employees by making them like him, believing that employees may work harder (a bit harder) for someone they like, a friend. Otherwise, forget motivation.

GENERAL PHILOSOPHY:

Believes that all people are good and worthy underneath it all, tends to be Pollyanna about the world, rationalizes negatives or ignores them entirely.

TRAINING:

Not a strong believer in training, believes that friendliness and co-operation in an organization will solve all problems, and should be cultivated.

TEAMWORK:

A lover of group activities and teamwork, but lacks the leadership qualities and resolve to build a strong, cohesive team.

PRODUCT:

A strong believer in quality first, please the customer regardless of cost or profit.

MAKING DECISIONS:

Does not like the responsibility of decisions, and does not want to make bold moves. Tries to get a consensus on all decisions, something all people will agree with.

CREATIVITY:	Tends to pay lip-service to innovation, but fails to implement programs . . . agrees with new ideas but buries them to avoid disturbing the status quo.
RESEARCH & DEVELOPMENT:	Only in a very conservative, limited manner, sticking to the improvement of current products, not developing new ones.
PUBLIC RELATIONS:	Important vehicle in building good will and in telling the world what a wonderful, caring company the Goodman Company is.
COMPETITION:	Avoids direct competition . . . fears conflict or hostility, often compromises with competitors for market share to avoid direct competition.
DELEGATING:	Likes to delegate work and responsibility, in order to avoid them . . . seldom follows up on projects, "I trust my employees to do right."
PEOPLE IN GENERAL:	People are more important than profit, they will work hard for you if they like you and approve of you.

OPERATIVE SKILLS:

SETTING OBJECTIVES:	Seldom sets goals which tax employees . . . often establishes goals and objectives that are discouragingly easy for more ambitious employees.
PLANNING STRATEGY:	Does not structure plans with care, not realistic. Believes everything will work itself out if everyone is caring and considerate.
FOLLOW UP:	Tends to be lax, fails to demand enough of employees. Over-praises minor achievements, forgives failures too quickly without proper analysis, sanctions incompetence.
DEVELOPING A COMPANY PHILOSOPHY:	Good at expressing an emotional, idealistic idea of the company's character, good at maintaining company quality and integrity. Usually poor at realistic profit objectives.
STANDARDS AND POLICY:	Lax enforcement of policy, loosely sets standards, conflicts of enforcing rules avoided.

AN OVERVIEW OF GARY GOODMAN...

FREEDOM FACTORS:

- DEPENDENT, LACKING OBJECTIVITY
- A STRICT CONFORMIST... ADDICTED TO APPROVAL AND SOCIAL STATUS
- A NON-ACTIVE AGENT ...PASSIVE

CREATIVE FACTORS:

- AT TIMES SPONTANEOUS AND OPEN (TO A DEGREE)
- EGO-CENTERED...LACKS PROBLEM SOLVING SKILLS, SELDOM INNOVATES, SEEKS SAMENESS & STABILITY

INNER-CONNECTION FACTORS:

- SELDOM A DEEP THINKER OR CONCEPTIONALIZER

LOVE FACTORS:

- VERY MUCH AFFECTION-ADDICTED...SEEKS WARMTH BY GIVING IT

PERCEPTION FACTORS:

- FILTERS OUT NEGATIVES ...AVOIDS FACING UNPLEASANT REALITIES ...SEES ONLY THE "GOOD"

HUMANISTIC FACTORS:

- LIKES PEOPLE, VERY TOLERANT AND IDEALISTIC
- GOOD SENSE OF HUMOR...CAN LAUGH AT HIMSELF
- APPRECIATES THE WORLD AROUND HIM IN AN AESTHETIC SENSE
- CONDONES NEGATIVE PEOPLE, COPES THROUGH APPEASEMENT

POINTS TO REMEMBER:

—PROBE GARY'S quick and easy agreements... uncover his submerged reservations and disagreements.

—PRESENT ONLY the necessary supporting data for a proposition, do not inundate Gary with details and options.

—DON'T ATTEMPT to be exploitive.

—PERMIT GARY to establish favorable communication circumstances, visit with him for awhile.

—RECOGNIZE AND BE CONSIDERATE of Gary's needs for security, approval, and esteem.

—IF YOU HAPPEN to be a passive/warm type, seek to become more comfortably assertive, <u>rather than</u> less compassionate and considerate.

REFERENCES:

Abraham Maslow: <u>MOTIVATION & PERSONALITY</u>, Harper & Row, New York, 1954

Manuel J. Smith: <u>WHEN I SAY NO, I FEEL GUILTY</u>, Dial Press, New York, 1975

William and Marguerite Beecher: <u>BEYOND SUCCESS AND FAILURE, WAYS TO SELF-RELIANCE AND MATURITY</u>, Pocket Books, New York, 1975

Harry Browne: <u>HOW I FOUND FREEDOM IN AN UNFREE WORLD</u>, Avon Books, New York, 1974

W. Hugh Missildine: <u>YOUR INNER CHILD OF THE PAST</u>, Simon and Schuster, New York, 1981

W. Hugh Missildine and Lawrence Galton: <u>YOUR INNER CONFLICTS, HOW TO SOLVE THEM</u>, Simon and Schuster, New York, 1974

Buzzota, Lefton and Sherberg: <u>EFFECTIVE SELLING THROUGH PSYCHOLOGY: DIMENSIONAL SALES AND SALES MANAGEMENT STRATEGIES</u>, Wiley Interscience, New York, 1972

"OLD FASHIONED MANAGEMENT IS FAR MORE DANGEROUS THAN OUTMODED EQUIPMENT"

Y OU ENTER the remarkable company of Mike Mature. It is unique, unlike any company you have ever seen before.

Mike's company, the Maximum-Effort Sporting Goods Company, is a national chain. Here at the home office, all the chief executive personnel and their staffs are housed under the same roof.

As a matter of fact, the home office is one giant, spacious room. There are very few barriers or partitions. In one corner is the "office" of Mike Mature. Actually, it is more of an "area" than an office.

Mike is seated at a large table, rather than a desk. Mike beckons you to approach.

You sit down at the desk, or rather the table, of Mike Mature. There is no dramatic lighting, no front, no props of "power."

Mike offers you a cup of coffee. He is relaxed, and has an amused warm smile. He likes what he is doing. He begins to talk to you about his company.

"Did you know that I once worked for Harry Haight? He told me back then that I had a great deal to learn.

"Harry was right about *that* – and I am still learning. He believed that I was naive about people. Perhaps. Certainly, I expect a great deal from people.

"I don't try to regiment or structure certain people very much. Phil Fullment is a good example. Phil structures his own methods of reaching company goals; he is excellent at doing it. But, of course, Ron Remote and George Gentle require rather clearly defined workloads and very specific goals.

"Contrary to some people's beliefs, we do not operate on exactly an honor system here. All employees share in the company profits. In fact, somewhat in the manner of the Japanese, a considerable amount of their pay is based upon our unusually high quarterly bonuses. If someone sluffs off, he or she is taking money right out of their co-worker's pockets.

"Consequently, we have a remarkable degree of employee enforcement of work standards here ... both in quality and in hours worked.

"Abraham Maslow once said that the companies of the future will face dramatically changing circumstances. Those companies which attempt to hang on to old-fashioned ideas about people are as doomed as those which attempt to keep obsolete equipment.

"In fact, my judgment is that old-fashioned management is far more dangerous than outmoded equipment.

"A company unwilling to become enlightened about the cultivation of human resources is a modern dinosaur ... and it is only a matter of time until it becomes extinct.

"But, go on, enjoy yourself. Look around to your heart's content. If you need anything, give me a call."

8

MIKE MATURE...The Compassionate/ Assertive Boss

... How He Guides with Poise and Grace and How You Can Profit Most from His Nourishing Attitude

Y OU MAKE your way across the large room that houses the home office employees of the Maximum Effort Sporting Goods Company. From several desks away you spot Paula Pushey – a scowling woman of about 32. "Oh-oh," you think, " a Ruthless/Aggressive personality."

MIKE MATURE . . . AS SEEN THROUGH THE EYES OF PAULA PUSHEY

After you are settled in Paula's office area she begins to unfold the story of an unusual relationship – her relationship with Mike Mature.

"Mike is a tough customer . . . Don't let anybody tell you different. In the clutch he can dish it out and take it with the best of them.

"I must admit that I respect the guy's strength. Anything I can't stand is a male with no guts.

157

"I'VE BEEN ABLE TO TALK TO MIKE..."

"Mike is a no-nonsense businessman, not like the average wishy-washy pussy cats I've worked for in the past. You know, when I first joined this company I thought he would be a pushover.

"I guess I sorta was testing. Wow! He came down on me! Not loud or overbearing, but he can look you in the eye and make you know who is boss in ten seconds flat!

"And yet I've been able to talk to Mike...I think he really respects my point of view. He must recognize my abilities, my talents and my strengths.

"When we had that little showdown, I had the feeling he would have fired me if I had not backed down.

"I guess I can sum it up this way – this company is OK...at least it's better than most. I feel I'm getting a lot out of working here.

"I respect Mike. There is a quiet confidence in him that you can't easily shake. How can you help but respect a guy like that?"

As you leave Paula, you make a mental note. She is probably far more productive in Mike's company than she would be in an immature company. She actually seems content, a rare state for such a personality. You realize that Mike has to walk a tightrope to get the maximum performance from Paula. He must be strong enough to be the boss, but considerate of her deep ego and independence needs.

Your next stop is the accounts receivable area and Ron Remote.

Ron is a typical Hostile/Timid individual. He seems to want to avoid the interview, but he is trapped in the open offices of the Maximum Effort Sporting Goods Company.

MIKE MATURE, AS SEEN THROUGH
THE EYES OF RON REMOTE

"Well, Mike probably told you that I'm a problem, didn't he?"

You assure Ron that Mike said nothing about him.

"Well, OK. The reason I said that is because I spent a few hours with Mike talking things over last week. I had a run-in with that bitch, Paula Pushey.

"Mike is about the only boss I've ever trusted. You know, most bosses would stab you in the back as quick as look at you. But Mike is different, so far.

"The story I get is that he really put Paula Pushey in her place. Somebody needed to clip her wings.

"I tried to tell Mike that Paula was putting stuff in the direct mailings that was exaggerated, not the copy he had approved. We were having trouble collecting from some accounts because they felt we had oversold our ability to deliver. As soon as Mike understood my position, he was sympathetic.

"But Paula got wind of what I had done and came down to my department and started a war.

"It took a while for Mike to smooth things out. I hear he did a number on Paula, but I didn't get to gloat long. He put it on me also. He was fair, I guess.

"If Mike believed that there were any hard feelings still affecting the work he would move on the situation fast.

"You know, once I had 3 people working for me here. Now I'm really a one-man department. I like it. Mike said I would be happier with a clear-cut assignment, so he switched me with George Gentle. All I need do is send out form letters and refer difficult cases to Mike.

"Mike kind of structures me tightly, I guess. But at least I know where I stand.

"I was amazed when Mike came down the other day and talked to me for so long. I honestly felt he cared about me and my feelings.

"In a rotten world like this, I have to admit that there are a few square shooters – after working for Mike."

After your session with Ron Remote, you are impressed with the fact that he's more content and more productive than any of the other Hostile/Timid types you have met in the other companies.

Your next stop is the Warm/Timid George Gentle, in customer relations.

MIKE MATURE AS SEEN THROUGH THE EYES OF GEORGE GENTLE

As you might have guessed, George is smiling as you approach.

"Hello! How are you?" George says. "Are you enjoying your stay here? Can I get you a cup of coffee?

"Isn't this a wonderful company? Just one happy family! Mike is the most splendid of bosses.

"True, he gave me a scare at first. When Mike took over the company, I was afraid he was a bit overbearing . . . you know, he made so many changes.

"I was in charge of accounts receivable then, and I hated it. I felt so sorry for the people who fell behind in their payments. Mike talked to me at length about my job, and really listened to me. He switched me to customer relations.

"I love it!

"Mike is unlike any other boss I've known. He doesn't tell me: 'Be assertive! Be tough!' But he does demand that I be businesslike and efficient.

"MIKE IS HARD TO FOOL ."

"Mike did caution me to clean up my paper work, and to take a course in management if I wanted to stay here. He said this very nicely but I really think he meant it.

"I heard Paula Pushey say that Mike is tough, but he really isn't . . . He is a strong man, but he is extremely considerate, really.

"I consider Mike a friend; but don't get me wrong. I'll never go into his office unprepared with facts and figures again! Boy he got on me for talking in generalities and not having my facts straight!

"Mike is hard to fool."

Again, you have the impression of productivity, of an immature person motivated by just the right amount of pressure on his sensitive areas.

Your last stop is with Phil Fullment, the Compassionate/Assertive Director of Merchandising for the Maximum Effort Sporting Goods Company.

MIKE MATURE AS SEEN THROUGH THE EYES OF PHIL FULLMENT

The area of Phil Fullment is a buzz of activity, focus, and purpose. Phil is a youngish 50, and he seems to be enjoying himself.

"Let me tell you," says Phil, "how much I like my work. I've greatly benefitted from the experience of working here.

"Mike enjoys new and innovative approaches, provided they have been thoroughly thought through. He has no big ego hangups, unlike 95% of the entrepreneurs I have known. I'm really free to conceive ideas and execute them to the best of my ability, with one important qualification.

"I must have the facts. Mike regards factual preparation as the single most important criteria for action. He calls it making yourself 'free to fly,' much as a pilot must have a thorough awareness of the technicalities of flying and completely check out his plane before he is truly 'free to fly.'

"I OVERHEARD MIKE QUOTE WALT DISNEY THE OTHER DAY."

"Another thing about Mike is that he emphasizes that the customer is 'king.' He insists that all merchandise be customer-oriented, specifically designed and intended to fill a need of the customer.

"When I decide to take an important action, I first present the plans for it to Mike. Mike is thorough in grilling me about my decisions. I always prepare myself carefully for these sessions.

Often I have *dropped* plans before discussing them with Mike, because I discovered a negative that I had previously overlooked.

"Mike is a pleasure to communicate with, when I am really prepared. He really listens to me and he is clear in his own ideas.

"I am flexible in my marketing effort because Mike encourages me to be. He expects me to have knowledge about the activities of competitors, on a regular and organized schedule. We are seldom surprised by the activities of our competition.

"We also study our suppliers, and continually update and revise our merchandise lineup.

"I've discovered Mike to be one of the few bosses I can relax around. He has a sense of humor, and can even laugh at himself now and then.

"Mike doesn't go for a lot of phony flim-flam about product, nor does he permit office politics to flourish around here.

"I believe the company's philosophy is clear to everyone. Mike communicates company goals to us, and he invites our participation in the dynamics of establishing those goals.

"When he first came here he tried to institute a new procedure that would expedite paper flow. No one thought it would work. We fought the idea. We argued. We showed him how this could not work. Finally he took us in his office and said: 'I now know why this program will not work. Everyone has given me ample reasons for its impracticality. Now I want every manager to go home and think of several reasons why it *will* work. No negatives are to be presented. Everyone report for a meeting at 8 a.m. Monday with at least two *positive reasons* why this system WILL work.'

"Well, lo and behold if that didn't convince most of us. We had actually developed a plan that would expedite his ideas, and it *DID* work! Naturally it worked – we helped create it!

"We also have one of the best profit-sharing plans I have ever seen. Mike really has a team effort here, no kidding. He never – I mean *never* – violates the chain of command, no matter what. He delegates authority and responsibility in appropriately balanced amounts.

"He has a strong belief in training, and he believes in cultivating human resources.

"I overheard Mike quote Walt Disney the other day as saying: 'Treat people as though they were pure gold; give them your best shot in life, and they will come through for you . . .'

"Mike does this. He really *sees* people and *hears* them. He pays careful attention to every contact . . . even the janitor.

"Mike is a great boss. I admire him."

THE REAL MIKE MATURE

To a greater degree than any other boss we have studied, Mike *is what he appears to be.* He achieves success with each personality type; he is a masterful leader.

Mike is more flexible than any of the other bosses. He can be, under the appropriate circumstances, as tough and aggressive as Harry Haight, as warm and friendly as Gary Goodman, or as cool and withdrawn as Fred Fridgide.

People like Mike are more unique and diverse than immature people. The Compassionate/Assertive type is a *self-actualizer: a person who is in the never-ending process of "becoming," of "developing." Self-actualization is a process, not a destination.*

Mike's flexibility is due to natural or developed affection for people, rather than a deliberate attempt to manipulate or get along. He really likes most people. He has little difficulty adjusting to people's personalities.

Mike's encouragement of creativity is rooted in his own confidence, his self-esteem, and his own creative tendencies. Mike never gives responsibility without authority; he delegates the proper measure of guidance and structure.

Mike believes in team effort; he understands the principles of synergism*. He encourages genuine two-way communication.

Mike leads by superlative example; his standards are high. He understands people who wish to grow and improve.

Of all the bosses, Mike achieves the greatest productivity and success.

---

*Synergism means the behavior of system-parts working together can be greater than the sum of the parts. For example, chrome-nickel steel is made from (basically) chromium, nickel, iron and carbon. The tensile strength of chromium is about 70,000 psi (pounds per square inch), iron 60,000 psi, nickel about 80,000 psi, carbon and minor constituents about 50,000 psi. Add all these together and you get 260,000 psi. Yet the actual casting tensile strength of chrome-nickel steel is 350,000 psi . . . far greater than the sum of its parts!

THE MASKS OF MIKE MATURE

Mike does not use masks in the conscious way that immature bosses do. His flexibility is such that he really doesn't need to use masks. He can quite spontaneously and naturally be warm, aggressive, or cold, as the situation dictates.

However, as with any other human being, Mike can be pushed too far. He can reach a state of frustration, and slip into an involuntary frustration behavior. At such times he will act like Harry Haight, and, if further frustrated, Fred Fridgide.

WHILE IN THESE FRUSTRATION BEHAVIOR-PATTERNS, Mike may tend to use masks as Harry or Fred would. In this particular "mode" Mike is not a true C/A person, but is really (temporarily) a Harry Haight or a Fred Fridgide.

The most honest and mature people use masks now and then. The best of us have a little Harry Haight, Fred Fridgide and Gary Goodman in us.

FOUR POSITIVE TACTICS FOR DEALING WITH MIKE MATURE

Mike is the one kind of boss you can be up-front with; you can be candid and direct with him.

Harry has a gigantic ego problem that you must work around. Fred requires great skill in approach and in communications. Gary is difficult to keep focused on the matter at hand.

Mike, however, is a genuine two-way communicator. He will listen as well as talk. Mike will not attempt to extract ego food from every situation in the manner Harry does.

Unlike Fred and Gary, Mike will make strong growth decisions instead of safety decisions. He will back you up and will keep his word. The "tactics" that follow are basic suggestions for getting the most from a *healthy environment,* which should be appropriate words to describe your working conditions under Mike.

TACTIC #1: TALK IN TERMS OF PROFIT

Profit is the lifeblood of any business.

A mature business has a purpose and provides a service in exchange for a fair profit. No business can survive without profit.

Ideas should be presented to Mike with the realistic profit necessity considered. Not all ideas will yield immediate profit, some are long range. Some do not directly result in a bottom line improvement. But, in each case, your awareness of profit should be expressed.

In your important communications with Mike include references to profit, as well as service motives.

WHY is what you are doing or proposing important to your company? What tangible benefits will be enjoyed? How will it save money? Make personnel more productive?

Most ideas are rejected by companies because they are presented as *expenses,* as costing money. Because the ultimate benefits and dividends are not clearly expressed, many worthy programs are scrubbed.

In summary, put real substance into your communications with a man like Mike Mature. You will note that his ideas contain substance and originality, and he appreciates similar qualities in yours.

TACTIC #2: BE INNOVATIVE

Nothing impresses Mike more than creative, innovative people. Harry Haight distrusts creativity. (He believes creativity is the art of concealing your sources.) Fred totally rejects new ideas; Gary fears innovation and can't follow through on new courses of action.

Mike Mature loves new ideas. He gives people credit for their ideas, and he rewards their creativity.

Stretch your mind. Can't you think of a way to do it better? Quicker? Should it be done at all?

Submit your ideas in writing, complete with facts, figures and supporting data. This is the professional way, and this will appeal to Mike.

TACTIC #3: KNOW YOUR FACTS!

Do your homework. Be prepared for specific questions with specific, concrete answers. *Anticipate.*

Know your company's product. Know your competition. Be organized. Be prepared.

AND – BE FLEXIBLE.

For example, Mike appreciates factual statements of this nature:

"This program will reduce our breakage costs by 25%, based upon data from the packing company."

YET, Mike could reply in this manner:

"I understand, but our breakage is now low enough, and this program costs considerably more than our current program."

To which your masterful reply might be:

"Mike, my data does not agree with this assertion. Morley's (a major competitor) has 17% less freight damage than we have and pays more for their packaging than this proposal recommends. I believe our current system costs us profits."

Harry Haight would violently attack such a threat to his ego (that is, if you seemed to know more about some phase of his business than he did!). Fred would shrug the facts off; Gary would be befuddled by the data.

Mike, however, respects the direct, self-assertive approach. Use it, but be respectful and be right.

TACTIC #4: LEARN TO BECOME A PERSON LIKE MIKE

In your own life and in your area of operation in your company, model yourself after Mike.

Ask yourself: "When I *arrive*, when I become the world-class person I aspire to become, how will I run my life? Will I still procrastinate and avoid problems? Or will I be confident, organized and on top of things?"

Begin to run your life *now* the way you will then. If you are going to become a great writer, or artist, or fashion buyer, or entrepreneur, *begin to act like one today!*

First BE. Then the strength to DO will follow.

Study the "games" that winners play in the last section of this book. Play like a winner and you will progress geometrically and synergistically in Mike's Company, and for the rest of your career.

BOSS: MIKE MATURE

VARIATIONS: INFINITE

TYPE: COMPASSIONATE/
ASSERTIVE

GENERAL SKILLS:

LEADERSHIP: A strong balanced leader, mature, compassionate and warm. Yet assertive, optimistic and confident.

COMMUNICATION: A two-way communicator, listens "actively." Clearly and passionately conveys his own ideas. Sensitive to all kinds of verbal and non-verbal communication from others.

MOTIVATIONAL ABILITIES: A flexible motivator who has a "sixth sense about people." Knows what will motivate them and inspire them, leads by superlative example.

GENERAL PHILOSOPHY:

Has a realistic, cognitively competent view of the world ... sees flaws and faults and also opportunities and potentials.

TRAINING: Believes in initial training as an investment and continuing enrichment programs for personnel and himself.

TEAMWORK: Has a keen sense of balance in the role of teamwork, uses a mixture of strength and a masterful melding of personalities toward common goals.

PRODUCT: Produces a product or service that fills a need at a realistic price, and of appropriate quality ... Stands behind his product or service and promotes it aggressively.

MAKING DECISIONS: Utilizes the feedback of others and carefully considers the opinions of the group when making decisions that will affect their welfare and environment.

CREATIVITY: Quite creative and very encouraging of the creative process. Compassionate/assertive companies always, without fail or exception, produce or serve in a unique and creative manner.

168

RESEARCH & **DEVELOPMENT:**	Considered very important. Tries to look at a product or service as a competitor would and asks: "If I were a competitor, what would I do to surpass my product?" Then Mike does it himself.
PUBLIC RELATIONS:	Feels a deep responsibility to the community and a need to express this concern by projecting an accurate image of his company to the world.
COMPETITION:	Enjoys a healthy competition but is largely in competition with himself. How well is he actually doing relative to his potentials?
DELEGATING:	Realistically delegates responsibility and authority in appropriate balance... Believes in training employees by giving them responsibility.
PEOPLE IN **GENERAL:**	Believes realistically in the positive potential of all normal human beings... Tries to help workers develop and mature in a nourishing, supportive atmosphere.

OPERATIVE SKILLS:

SETTING **OBJECTIVES:**	Encourages employees to participate in the goal-setting procedure. Develops goals which involve and motivate employees directly.
PLANNING **STRATEGY:**	Develops long range (5-year),medium range (1-year),and short range strategies that are based upon realistic data and input. Shares with his employees his overall method to achieve goals and objectives.
FOLLOW UP:	Consistent and regular... knows the best employee performance rating is the one given right after the moment of execution.
DEVELOPING A **COMPANY** **PHILOSOPHY:**	Formulates his company's philosophy with a realistic and toughly compassionate self-enlightened technique... Believes in sharing the responsibility for success and profits from success with employees.
STANDARDS AND **POLICY:**	Adheres honestly to standards he sets and insists that others do the same... Standards and policies are ideals to be lived up to, not control techniques.

AN OVERVIEW OF MIKE MATURE...

FREEDOM FACTORS:

- TRANSCENDENCE: ABLE TO RISE ABOVE THE DUST OF THE BATTLE
- A NON-CONFORMING CONFORMIST: A STRANGER IN A STRANGE LAND WHO CONFORMS TO MOST SOCIAL GRACES WITH A SENSE OF AMUSEMENT
- INDEPENDENCE: A LONER WHO LIKES OTHER PEOPLE
- AN ACTIVE AGENT: A KNIGHT AMONG PAWNS

INNER-CONNECTION FACTORS:

- A FEARLESS CHILD OF THE UNIVERSE WITH A RICH INNER LIFE

COGNITIVE FACTORS:

- ABLE TO SEE AND GET ALONG WITH THINGS AS THEY ARE

LOVE FACTORS:

- A FEW VERY DEEP AND CLOSE RELATIONSHIPS OF SUPREME VALUE

CREATIVE FACTORS:

- SPONTANEITY: A FREE-ACTING AGENT WITHOUT DESTRUCTIVE IMPULSIVENESS
- CREATIVITY: VERY STRONG, SOMETIMES AWESOME POWERS OF INNOVATIVE THINKING AND ACTION
- PROBLEM-SOLVING: SOLVES THE PROBLEMS OF LIFE WITHOUT EGO HANG-UPS

HUMANISTIC FACTORS:

- A CHILDLIKE ACCEPTANCE OF SELF, PEOPLE AND THINGS
- IDEALISM: A QUIXOTE-LIKE VISION OF LIFE AS IT *SHOULD* BE, AND A CONVICTION THAT IT *COULD* BE THAT WAY
- HUMOR: A FREE, OPEN AND HEALTHY SENSE OF HUMOR, INCLUDING THE ABILITY TO LAUGH AT HIMSELF
- APPRECIATION: SEES THE WORLD AS AN EVER-FRESH, WONDROUS CREATION
- DEMOCRACY: A COLOR-BLIND, STATUS-IGNORING COMPANION TO OTHERS
- BIG BROTHERHOOD: ESTABLISHES CARING RELATIONSHIPS WITH LESS ADJUSTED HUMAN BEINGS

POINTS TO REMEMBER:

LET'S VISIT AWHILE ABOUT THIS PROBLEM . . .

— **STRIVE** to become a mature, self-actualizing person like Mike.

— **LEARN** to talk to Mike in terms of **PROFIT** and mutual self-interest.

— **KNOW YOUR FACTS** . . . but be flexible . . . be ready to revise in the light of new data.

— **BE INNOVATIVE** and bold . . . use your creativity with assertiveness . . . Mike will not feel threatened.

⬤ THE COMPASSIONATE/ASSERTIVE ACTUALIZER IS: A self-reliant, self-contained, dynamically evolving entity who receives and processes data with relative accuracy and who operates creatively and productively with the maximum of internal and external efficiency in the psychological arena of life.

NOTE: THE MATERIAL ON THESE TWO PAGES IS BASED UPON ABRAHAM MASLOW'S FAMOUS PAPER: *Self-Actualizing People: a Study in Psychological Health.* This paper can be found in the book, *Motivation and Personality.* (See reference page.)

REFERENCES:

Abraham Maslow: <u>MOTIVATION AND PERSONALITY</u>, Harper and Row, New York, 1954

Abraham Maslow: <u>THE FARTHER REACHES OF HUMAN NATURE</u>, Viking Press, New York, 1973

Buzzotta, Lefton and Sherburg: <u>EFFECTIVE SELLING THROUGH PSYCHOLOGY, DIMENSIONAL SALES & SALES MANAGEMENT</u>, Wiley Interscience, New York, 1972

George A. Steiner: <u>STRATEGIC PLANNING, WHAT EVERY MANAGER MUST KNOW</u>, Macmillan Publishing Company, New York, 1981

Robert R. Blake and Jane Srygley Mouton: <u>THE VERSATILE MANAGER, A GRID PROFILE</u>, Dow-Jones Irwin, Homewood, Illinois, 1980

Dr. Thomas Gordon: <u>LET: LEADER EFFECTIVENESS TRAINING</u>, Wyden Books, 1977

Carl R. Boll: <u>EXECUTIVE JOBS UNLIMITED</u>, Macmillan Publishing Company, New York, 1968

Leonard R. Sayles: <u>LEADERSHIP: WHAT EFFECTIVE MANAGERS REALLY DO AND HOW THEY DO IT</u>, McGraw-Hill, New York, 1979

William Ouchi: <u>THEORY Z: HOW AMERICAN BUSINESS CAN MEET THE JAPANESE CHALLENGE</u>, Addison-Wesley Publishing Company, Reading, Massachusetts, 1981

Bob Thomas: <u>WALT DISNEY . . . AN AMERICAN ORIGINAL</u>, Simon & Schuster, New York, 1976

R. Buckminster Fuller: <u>SYNERGETICS</u>, Macmillan Publishing Company, New York, 1975

PART IV

THE FIVE DEADLY GAMES THAT BLOCK THE SELF-ACTUALIZATION PROCESS...

and Five Ways to Banish Them from Your Life Forever

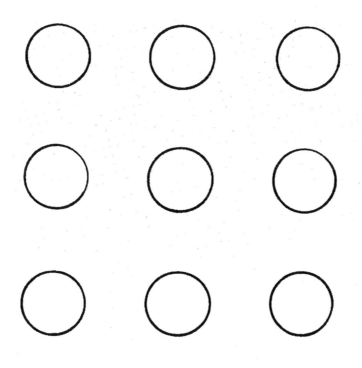

B EFORE YOU go on, try this little puzzle. The object of the game is to connect the nine circles with four straight lines, without lifting your pencil or pen from the paper. Please give it a try before you continue.

Did you succeed?
HERE is the correct solution:

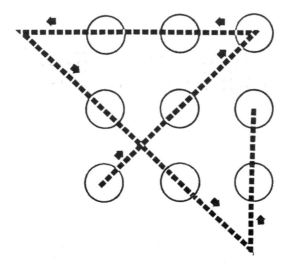

If you are like most people, your attempt looked something like this:

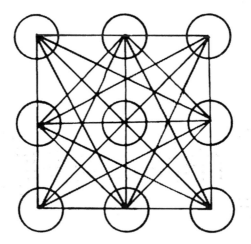

The puzzle cannot be solved in this way. That is, if you stay *within the area bounded by the circles,* you'll never find the solution. Instead, you will create a "game without end."

To solve the puzzle you must go *out* of the area that is bounded by the circles. Yet, very few people discover the solution. Almost everyone stays within the circle area, even though there is no rule that restricts them to this area.

Try as they may, no matter how patient they are, or how hard they exert themselves, this self-imposed rule will cause people to fail at the game.

Many people, really most people, live their lives restricted by similar self-imposed rules. And, worse than this, they believe the rules are *real* and cannot be changed.

> "…it obviously makes a difference whether we consider ourselves as pawns in a game whose rules we call reality or as players of the game who know that the rules are real only to the extent that we have created them, and we can change them."[*]

So it is that many people live lives that are "games without end." These people endure grey, boring, meaningless existences because they are trapped in a circle game of their own creation. They don't have the strength to break out, and they fear they don't have the strength to find happiness outside of their own little area of misery.

But let's stretch your mind further. Imagine connecting the circles with just THREE lines in the same manner.

Is it possible?

[*]Paul Watzlawick, John Weakland, Richard Fisch: CHANGE: PRINCIPLES OF PROBLEM FORMATION AND PROBLEM RESOLUTION, pg. 26, W.W. Norton & Company, Inc., New York, 1974.

Yes, unless you again impose a rule on yourself that makes it impossible:

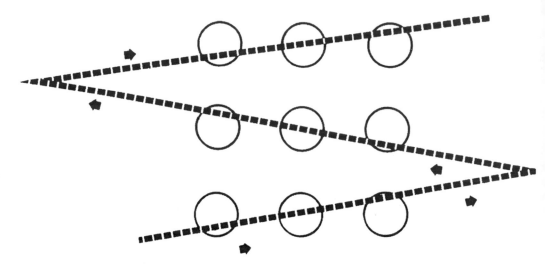

Naturally, circles have dimension. So the new solution works. But let us give you another "impossible" task – can you connect all the circles with a single pencil line in ONE stroke?

You can if you had a pencil with a giant, flat piece of lead in it!

In much the same manner of the circle game, the limitations and restrictions of life are self-imposed. Individuals postulate into existence their own timidness, lack of resolution and stupidity.

For you, the difference between winning and losing in the game of life may be simply the kind of rules you play by.

In this section we are going to show you five "games without end" that nearly all employees play. Each is a destructive and restrictive game.

We will show you how to change the rules and break out. The information you'll read was gathered over the last 20 years. The solutions have been tested in real life, and they work.

Your boss, and everyone else you know will soon wonder what's "gotten into you." (The interesting thing is that nothing "got into you," it was right there inside of you all the time!)

THE ODDS ARE TOO GREAT AGAINST THE EMPLOYEE!

If life is a game, it is a game that most employees lose. The odds are too great against the employee. The boss has all the advantages; the rules favor him.

One reason for the boss's advantage is the fact that he usually has a *goal*, and most employees do not. The boss most often has a greater degree of commitment, conviction, purpose and will power.

On the other hand the employee usually vacillates and compromises. He does things he really doesn't believe in, and he fails to do the things he wants to do.

The average employee lacks a goal, a reason, a purpose, a burning resolve. He plays the game by rules that keep him in a sleepwalking stupor.

The employee lacks will. His *heart* and his *head are not trying to do the same thing*. His heart is one place and his head is another.

Surely all employees want love, success, appreciation, and money. Yet many endure painful, hopeless situations instead of striking out in new directions.

Most people are afraid to go out of the area bounded by their "circles."

So, instead of a bold new life, most employees endure grey, hopeless, no-win games without end.

"Someday I'll...", many employees say. But they never *do,* they only talk.

The solution to this dilemma is a new set of rules, a new way of life. These rules will seem uncomfortable at first, but that is only because they are so different. If you have been playing the games without end for a long time, you may have forgotten how fun and adventurous life can be.

Here are the five most common and most destructive games that 95% of humanity plays, and loses.

THE 5 GAMES "WITHOUT END" THAT LOSERS PLAY:

1. THE DRIFT-DELUSION GAME,
    or "Waiting for the Voice of God,"
    or "Someday I'll..."

2. THE MESSIANIC MISCONCEPTION,
    or "If only everybody would..."

3. THE PHONY-LOYALTY GAME,
    or "My company, 'tis of Thee..."

4. COMPETITIVE-ROBOT TREADMILL GAME,
    or "How much money does he make?"

5. THE DIVINE MISERY OF MARTYRDOM,
    or "Look What They've Done to My Soul."

Now we are going to discuss each game, and for each we'll offer a nourishing substitute, a brand new set of rules.

REFERENCES:

Paul Watzlawick, John Weakland and Richard Fisch: CHANGE, PRINCIPLES OF PROBLEM FORMATION AND PROBLEM RESOLUTION, W.W. Norton Company, Inc., New York, 1974

Robert S. De Ropp: THE MASTER GAME, Dell Publishing Company, New York, 1968

W.W. Bartley III: WERNER ERHARD, THE TRANSFORMATION OF A MAN, THE FOUNDING OF EST, Clarkson N. Potter Co., New York, 1978

I BEGAN TO REALIZE THAT MAX WAS INTIMIDATING US ...

THE POWER of definite purpose, especially when used against the average employee, is overwhelming.

This was demonstrated to me several years ago when I worked for a particularly difficult and aggressive boss, a guy we'll call Max.

Max seemed to dominate any room he was in. Even though most people found him to be shallow, obnoxious and egoistic, they had to admit that he had an impressive "presence."

One summer Max took one of his rare vacations. While he was gone the office seemed pleasant and placid. When Max was due to return, I felt an unwilling, growing anxiety in myself. I also sensed fear in the other executives and employees.

Max came back like a buzz-saw – all tanned and fresh and ready to take on the world. While he was gone, I really tried to figure out what it was that made him so charismatic. Now that he was back, the secret still eluded me.

The first thing Max did was to call a staff meeting.

I watched Max as he answered questions, laughed, frowned, and made decisions with animated grace and ease. It began to dawn on me how he contrasted with the timid employees who surrounded his desk.

I began to realize that Max was intimidating us.

Max exuded confidence and dedication. The rest of us seemed to be on the defensive. We coped and retreated; we were no match for Max.

You see, *Max had a clear idea of what he wanted to do,* and how he wanted to do it. We employees simply reacted to what he said and did.

Max jarred us out of our comfortable routines. *None of us were so absorbed with what we were doing that we were insulated from this interruption.*

I personally felt woefully inadequate as Max relentlessly pressed the initiative.

After we left Max's office, and were a safe distance away, the group suddenly came to life. There were groans and complaints about Max. The real feelings we had to conceal in front of Max came out.

As this group of passive humanity began to break up and trickle to their desks, I began to clearly see the meaning and value of purpose.

The difference between timid and unhappy employees and the driving, aggressive boss was now evident.

ATTITUDE. That was it.

We were drifting, asleep, deluded. Max was goal-directed, alert, and realistic. Max had the *initiative* over his life and his environment.

We were part of the mediocre multitudes. We were willing victims of the DRIFT-DELUSION.

The "DRIFT-DELUSION"

The Game of Procrastinators...
How to Positively Cure it

T HE DRIFT-DELUSION DECLARATION:
"I am keeping my talent, my real enthusiasm, and my sincere commitment on hold until I discover what it is that I really want to do, or until the heavens open up and God speaks to direct me to some noble endeavor of supreme magnitude."

This is a false belief. It destroys more talent and potential and keeps more people asleep than any other belief I know.

THE DRIFT-DELUSION is the opium of mediocrity.

This belief causes you to be passive; it insulates you from the daily adventure of life.

The process of holding back and avoiding commitment prevents you from interacting with the very dynamics that are necessary to help you create meaningful objectives.

When you keep your potentials in reserve, they will decay and eventually *they will disappear altogether.* Once gone, these potentials are gone forever.

To get anywhere in life you MUST have a goal that you believe in, are committed to, and are dedicated to achieve.

Some people say: "Oh, I would like to have a goal to believe in, but I just don't know what I really want to do."

Please, DON'T EVER SAY THIS. It is not true. You DO know what you want to achieve.

If nothing else, you know you want to find your goal! This in itself is a goal, and a very difficult one. You must work very hard to achieve it. *Yes, you do know what you want.* You want to find your purpose. You've wanted to do this for a long time. You simply have not worked with all your resolve and dedication long enough to find it.

If you can't really work hard to discover your goal in life, what makes you think you'd work hard if you knew what it was you "wanted to do?"

So it is that your boss is stronger than you are. He may have very limited and selfish objectives, but they are probably clear in his mind, and he is acting to achieve them.

You see: *An individual who believes deeply in a foolish or unworthy idea is stronger than an individual who half believes in some noble idea.*

So your first step is clear. You must banish from your mind forever the idea that you have plenty of time. You have nothing but NOW.

Next, you need to replace the DRIFT-DELUSION with a whole new set of rules, a fresh and nourishing concept. We will replace the DRIFT-DELUSION with its counterpart game, the NEXT-STEP STRATEGY.

• THE WINNER'S GAME: THE NEXT-STEP STRATEGY

• THE NEXT-STEP STRATEGY IS THE PROCESS OF MOVEMENT, NO MATTER HOW SLIGHT, IN THE DIRECTION YOU KNOW YOU SHOULD BE GOING.

THE
NEXT-STEP
STRATEGY:

"Today I will exert the very best there is in me to move toward the accomplishment of my own personal NEXT-STEP. This is the constructive step I have known for a long time I should take, but I continue to procrastinate and fail to act upon. Today I will begin movement toward that step so that the NEXT Next-Step can appear."

The NEXT-STEP STRATEGY works, because even though you may not have long-range completely-clear goals, you DO know what your next step *should* be. You've known it for some time.

If you are honest with yourself, you will admit that you do know of a step you should take, one that will take you in the DIRECTION you want to go. It may be a very modest step, but that does not matter. What matters is DIRECTION and MOVEMENT.

Applying the NEXT-STEP STRATEGY is tough. At the end of each day you must answer the admonition: "DID I *TELL* THEM WHAT I AM GOING TO DO TODAY, OR DID I *SHOW* THEM?"

The "next step" reduces your opinions to a manageable few. It provides the rules that will permit you to win the "game," if you are willing to venture out of the "circles," and dare the unknown.

The great psychiatrist Alfred Adler had a favorite saying: "Trust only movement." Often we can be confused by words and theories. But movement is an infallible gauge.

Movement feels good. When you are moving in the right direction you feel buoyant, confident, powerful. The INSTANT you stop, when you become afraid or dependent, the world turns grey. It is an unmistakable gauge; you can feel it.

Next-Step activity is movement and action. It lets you pour out into the world those qualities you have, the enthusiasm you've been holding back for some "big" moment.

That big moment is the eternal NOW.

Abraham Maslow referred to movement as the process of making courageous growth decisions. Each day, moment-by-moment, you are making decisions *to go back toward safety or forward toward growth.* To continue movement, you must choose "growth" over and over again; fear must be overcome over and over again.

Each growth decision, or each next-step action (no matter how modest) gives you an enlarged perspective. What you didn't see as a possibility yesterday becomes clear and alluring after a next-step progression.

Fresh options, once obscured in the shadows, are illuminated and attractive as you take yet another courageous step forward.

Revitalizing energy and power come only AFTER you take ACTION on a next-step decision. Energies are replaced after they are fearlessly poured out, not before. Act, and you shall have the power.

A decision has not been completed until it has been acted out.

YOUR OWN PERSONAL NEXT-STEP

Each step should be taken with confidence and composure. Do not become hysterical. Keep in mind a test I have found valuable.

Imagine in your mind a fine fall day, with crystal clear air and an incredibly blue sky with a few white clouds stuck to it. See the leaves, brilliant and colorful, floating by... smell the fresh cool air. THIS is the feeling, the touchstone that should accompany a next-step. It is a feeling of rightness, of grace.

You may decide upon a very ambitious next-step! It could be that you will decide your next-step is to *sit down* and *write down* what you expect to achieve by this time next year. (This single action of writing down your goals would immediately put you in the top ten percent of Americans! Only one individual in ten writes down goals!)

Your next-step may be modest, like cleaning out that work-room (at last!) so that you can begin in earnest to be a photo-grapher as you have always dreamed (or a painter, or a writer, or whatever). Whatever next-step you decide, do it. Your *very first* "NEXT-STEP" action is to WRITE IT DOWN.

If you fail to write your next-step and begin moving, you will soon fall to sleep again and go into "automatic." You will begin to drift again. A golden moment will be lost forever.

Try the NEXT-STEP STRATEGY for a single week. You'll accomplish more than you did all last month – maybe all last year!

Other people will not like what is happening to you at first. They prefer to stay asleep, and they want you to do the same. The boss will begin to look at you with more respect.

This is only the beginning.

POINTS TO REMEMBER:

MOST PEOPLE CAN'T WIN because they are using a different set of "rules" than the boss...

THE DRIFT-DELUSION is one of the most common reasons for failure of passive individuals...

● **THE NEXT-STEP STRATEGY** starts creative action and focus upon an objective... Remember that the <u>boss</u> has focus, if nothing else! You must acquire it also!

REFERENCES:

Abraham Maslow: <u>THE FARTHER REACHES OF HUMAN NATURE</u>, Viking Press, New York, 1979

Willard and Marguerite Beecher: <u>BEYOND SUCCESS AND FAILURE</u>, Pocket Books, New York, 1975

Dorthea Brande: <u>WAKE UP AND LIVE</u>, Cornerstone Library, Simon and Schuster, New York, 1974

Dr. George Weinburg: <u>SELF CREATION</u>, St. Martin's Press, New York, 1978

Joe Karpo: <u>THE LAZY MAN'S WAY TO RICHES</u>, Joe Karpo, Sunset Beach, California, 1973

Napoleon Hill: <u>THINK AND GROW RICH</u>, The Ralston Society, Cleveland, Ohio, 1945

"WHAT THE HELL DO YOU CARE?" THE OLD GUY FINALLY SAID . . .

MANY YEARS ago I worked for the Western Electric Company, which is a subsidiary of the Telephone Company.

I was an installer and tester of central office equipment, and I hated the job.

What I really wanted was to become an artist. I had written down my goal, planned my steps, and trained intensely.

Somehow I couldn't get an art job. Each night I studied and drew. Sometimes I would get up at 4:00 A.M. to practice. I made contacts in the art world and went on many job interviews.

Several of my co-workers at the phone company became aware of my ambition to become an artist. One older fellow was especially encouraging. He told me it was too late for him, but I still had a chance to "get out."

Because I was working full time at the Western Electric Company, and had been for eight years, I felt drawn into daily work competition with the other employees.

We competed for raises, prestige and recognition. Sometimes I would boil for weeks if I was passed over for a "merit raise."

One day I expressed resentment to my older co-worker about my failure to get a raise. To make matters worse, another man who was not nearly as competent as I had gotten a sizeable increase.

I went on and on talking about the "rotten company" to my captive audience. He looked at me impatiently. "What the hell do you care?" the old guy finally said.

"What do you mean, what do I care? Of course, I care!"

"Ain't you studying to become an artist?" he asked.

"Yes, but so what?"

"Well if you are serious about that, you know you'll be gone from here someday. *So, what does what he gets have to do with what you say you are, or what you're gonna be?*"

Lamely, I tried to say that I wanted to do the best I could while I was working for the Western Electric Company, but he didn't buy it. He simply shrugged his shoulders and walked away.

I had to face the facts. I had to be content with pursuing one goal at a time.

This realization lifted a great burden from me. I was free of a game I had created, the "MESSIANIC MISCONCEPTION," another game without end.

Once I accepted the responsibility of pursuing a single goal, it was not long before I was able to get my first art job. From that moment, I entered into a new world and never looked back.

10

The "MESSIANIC MISCONCEPTION" Trap...

...How to Avoid It and Keep Resolutely Focused Upon Your Goal

THE MESSIANIC MISCONCEPTION is very different from the Drift-Delusion.

As the DRIFT-DELUSION is a game for the passive majority of people, the MESSIANIC MISCONCEPTION is a self-defeating game for active, aggressive individuals.

Here is how it goes:

> **THE MESSIANIC MISCONCEPTION DECLARATION:**
> **"I can pursue my main goal and still have time and energy to compete with others, and to correct the methods and attitudes of the individuals and organizations with which I must deal."**

This idea is wrong. It is like advocating an attempt to catch two rabbits at the same time. (You may very well miss them both!)

Some of the people who practice the MESSIANIC MISCON-CEPTION accomplish things, but they never come near reaching their full potential.

I once knew a man who *could* have been one of the wealthiest professionals in the country – except for the fact that he went off on tangents.

This man, whom we will call Jerry Cohen, had wonderful talents and a deep desire to be wealthy and independent. In fact, Jerry was one of the few geniuses I've ever known.

I met Jerry in the autumn of his career. Jerry was still possessed of prodigious talent and intelligence. He had worked hard all his life, but the great material rewards he craved had never really come to him.

Jerry was busy with an idea service he had created for national magazines. It was a good service. Although there were problems to be solved, it had considerable potential.

Jerry poured a great deal of money, and a titanic effort into his service. Even so, it eventually failed.

The big reason it failed, in my judgment, was because Jerry could not stick on course; he wanted to *change the way magazines did business.*

Jerry once told me that his main objective with his business was to make a handsome profit. To achieve this he knew it was necessary to persuade his current subscribers (the magazines) into renewing their subscriptions to his service each year. He also would have to attract new subscribers.

Simple enough. Main objective: To make a good profit.

Then Jerry was invited to talk before a national convention of magazine editors. He shocked and alienated them. He began to attack his clients!

Jerry blasted the integrity of the magazine advertising rate structures; he heaped scorn on the space-salesmen for magazines; he deplored the complacency of magazine management.

Some of Jerry's ideas about magazine management were good ideas. And it was true that the magazine business seemed too set in its ways, too vulnerable.

"FIRST TIME ON A BOAT AND HE WANTED TO BE THE CAPTAIN!"

But Jerry's main objective was not to reform the magazine industry. It was to sell his service and make a profit.

If Jerry had set out to specifically change the way magazines did business, his actions would have been more appropriate. Instead, Jerry was selling a service, one that could only survive if it was able to mesh with the way magazines actually did business.

Soon Jerry's own business began to falter.

One day I ran across a significant passage in a book I was reading. I decided to show it to Jerry. The most important part read as follows:

> "Use things the way they are. Unless your specific... objective is to change the status quo, do not attempt to change the basic makeup of people, organizations, mores, policies, etc. Operate within existing structures. Instead of, for example, fighting bureaucracy, learn to use it for cover. If a man is an egoist, you won't be able to change him, but you will be able to communicate with him through his ego."*

"This makes sense!" Jerry said. We then had some discussion about working within the existing "system" of magazines. Jerry resolved to turn over a new leaf.

But it didn't last.

*PRESENTING TECHNICAL IDEAS: A Guide to Audience Communication by W.A. Mambert, pg. 13, John Wiley & Sons, Inc., New York, 1968

Before long Jerry was again attacking the methods and policies of magazines. He seemed to understand, intellectually, the principle of sticking to selling his own service.

But Jerry had ego needs that he could not overcome. He satisfied these needs by berating his bewildered clients until they began to desert him in droves.

Several years later I happened to have a conversation with a magazine editor who had once subscribed to Jerry's service. When the subject of Jerry came up, the executive began to bristle.

"Look," he said. "I've been in the magazine business for twenty-five years and I made money for my magazine each year. Jerry had no deep grasp of the magazine business, he was just a bright dilettante. First time on a boat and he wanted to be the captain!"

Like Jerry, many gifted people suffer from the MESSIANIC MISCONCEPTION. These people pursue "burning issues" and generally clutter their lives up with trivia.

The result is a game without end. There isn't any time left to do the *real work*.

Suppose you were going to take an automobile trip to some specific destination. You have just about enough gas and time to get there. No doubt you would select the shortest, most practical route.

But suppose you decided to take several side trips along the way. What if you began to dilly-dally and waste time . . . would this make sense?

Yet most people do exactly this. They act as though they had unlimited time and their energy was inexhaustible.

The achiever has the strongest incentive, the deepest sense of urgency, and takes the shortest road.

THE "MAIN-ISSUE" MAXIM

You can avoid the trap of the MESSIANIC MISCONCEPTION if you apply the proper cure. It has various names, but I call it the MAIN-ISSUE MAXIM.

THE MAIN-ISSUE MAXIM:

"Today I will exert all my effort to focus upon the MAIN ISSUE of my life, my NEXT-STEP, and will shun all ego food and ignore all unrelated issues. I will use existing systems, people and institutions to accomplish my objectives."

Now, the importance of having a clear goal is obvious. Otherwise the Main-Issue Maxim won't work. Above all, write down a goal that you really want, not one you think you should want.

Your heart and your head must be striving for the same purpose. There is no great secret of success that transcends this simple truth. *Make the desire of your mind the desire of your heart.*

The MAIN ISSUE MAXIM is especially valuable in freeing you from games without end when you are at work.

You'll find the most aggravating "problems" are those that have no bearing on your own personal main issue. They are usually someone else's main issue, or simply a bit of ego food you could really live without.

If you could see into the future and knew you were going toward an inevitable victory, *if you could know for certain success would crown your efforts, the MAIN-ISSUE MAXIM would be easy to apply.*

I eventually did reach my own goal of becoming an artist. If I could have seen into the future and known that this would happen, *it would have released tremendous energies in me that were being dissipated on competition and anxiety.*

When you feel muddled, apply the MAIN-ISSUE MAXIM and wait for the clarity to return before you go on.

Flow in quiet confidence, smoothly, crystal clear to your next step. You will begin to sense some interesting, subtle changes in people's attitudes as you go. People always make way for someone who knows where he is going.

Even a boss like Harry Haight is at a loss when dealing with a cool, detached "fanatic" who has a resolute fixed purpose. Not a word need be spoken, no effort to combat the boss need be made.

You are free of your boss's games.

POINTS TO REMEMBER:

USE THINGS THE WAY THEY ARE... unless your specific objective is to change the status quo, work within the system to reach your goal.

TO EACH DIVERSION, each allurement, burning issue, or ego-contest apply the **MAIN-ISSUE MAXIM WITH RUTHLESS HONESTY.**

201

REFERENCES:

W.A. Mambert: <u>PRESENTING TECHNICAL IDEAS</u>, John Wiley and Sons, Inc., New York, 1968

David Seabury: <u>THE ART OF SELFISHNESS</u>, Cornerstone Library, New York, 1973

Harry Browne: <u>HOW I FOUND FREEDOM IN AN UNFREE WORLD</u>, The Macmillan Company, New York, 1973

Robert S. De Ropp: <u>THE MASTER GAME</u>, Dell Publishing Company, New York, 1968

Dorthea Brande: <u>WAKE UP AND LIVE</u>, Cornerstone Library, Simon and Schuster, New York, 1978

Robert J. Ringer: <u>WINNING THROUGH INTIMIDATION</u>, Fawcett Crest, Greenwich, Connecticut, 1974

"MY COMPANY... 'TIS OF THEE..."

"MY GOD ... WHAT AM I DOING?" I THOUGHT

S EVERAL years ago someone mailed me a clipping of an article that appeared in a major newspaper. The story shocked me. It told of the bankruptcy of a company I had worked for in the early part of my advertising career.

In those days, this company (which I'll call Borkey and Sons) was one of the leading retailers in America.

I thought the company was the most awesome organization I had ever worked for. The officers held court in plush surroundings that were rich with the glitter and symbols of power.

The Borkey company had a clearly defined hierarchy; members of the Borkey family held all of the top exectuve jobs.

The Borkey family members were always addressed as "Mr. Alex," "Mr. John," "Miss Alice" and so on. It was a serious faux pas to address a family member as simply "Alex" or even "Mr. Borkey."

The plantation-style atmosphere did not really bother me at the time. Each morning I would carry my new briefcase across the broad parking lot, and the towering silhouette of the Borkey Building assured me that I was part of something that would go on forever.

To be sure, things were going well for the company. It dominated retail sales in the local market area, and the store's volume was growing. "Mr. John," the executive vice president of the company, assured me that one day I would be doing double-page full-color national magazine ads for the company as it spread from coast-to-coast.

I was an executive for the first time in my life – something I had never been before. I even had an employee working for me!

I had been with the firm for several months when I experienced my first company-wide function: the Borkey and Sons 39th Annual Dinner and Songfest.

Each year it was the custom to invite all the employees to a large hotel in the downtown area to have dinner, and listen to speeches by the Borkey family members. The evening was capped by a sing-along of traditional songs.

The event was more tedious than you can imagine. After dinner, the first speaker was the 70 year-old president, Alex Borkey. Following Alex, his son John Borkey spoke. There followed speeches by Carl (Alex's brother), William (Carl's son), and finally a few words by "Miss Alice," the older men's sister and the company treasurer.

Each speech was enthusiastically applauded, and each joke dutifully laughed at. After the elite had spoken, each of the lower-ranking executives in the audience stood and made a few glowing statements of praise for the family.

At last it was time for the songfest. The employees and the Borkey family exuberantly sang old songs like: *I Wanna Girl, Down by the Old Mill Stream, The Old Grey Mare, and other ditties.*

Later in the evening John made a special announcement. I remember it as though it was yesterday. John's voice boomed over the loudspeaker:

"Folks, I have a wonderful new song for us to sing. It was written by our own warehouseman, Jimmy Wilkerson. At least,

Jimmy sure wrote the words! You'll find copies of the song on the back of your sheets. Now, let's sing loud and clear!"

I turned over my song sheet, and sure enough, there were the lyrics that Jimmy had written. The title of the song was: *"MY COMPANY 'TIS OF THEE."* A note under the title read: "Sing to the tune of *MY COUNTRY 'TIS OF THEE."*

Dutifully, and loudly, we began to sing.

Fortunately, memory begins to dim here, and the lyrics of the song have been mercifully erased in my mind by time.

I do remember though, that all the employees sang the song, or at least pretended to sing it, while John Borkey enthusiastically led the chorus.

Yes, I sang.

About halfway through the song I suddenly looked around and thought: "My God! What am I doing?" I didn't know what was wrong at the time, but I had a feeling *something* was wrong.

Now I know what I was doing; I was adding to the egoistic euphoria of the Borkey family. I was playing the role of a loyal employee, pretending to have exaggerated *moral* obligations that I really did not feel.

I was trapped in that deadly game of passive losers: THE PHONY-LOYALTY GAME.

11

How To Quit Playing
THE "PHONY-LOYALTY"
GAME...

...And How to Align Yourself with Those Powers
that Will Help You Achieve Your Destiny

A RE YOU a loyal employee? Before you answer, consider this
situation: You are at work. It is late in the afternoon, and the
luster of the day has worn off. You are tired.

The phone rings.

A pleasant voice tells you: "I am the president of Acme Company. For some time I have been watching you. I think you are
an excellent employee, and I believe you are grossly underpaid.

"Would you like to work for me? We have the highest reputation for treating people fairly. I will double your salary, give you a
nice Cadillac to drive, a credit card, and an appropriate title
to go with your function.

"All you will need to do is exactly what you are doing now, or modify it as you wish. Would you care to have dinner with me and at least discuss the possibility?"

Would you take him up on the offer? *Of course you would. So would any other sane person.*

And – all other factors being equal, if you were offered double the salary you are making now, double your current benefits and prestige for doing exactly what you are doing now, you'd jump at it.

Oh, there may be some cosmic duty that might prevent a common sense move like this, but it is unlikely. Surely you would not stay on at half-pay for loyalty reasons alone.

When this situation was posed to my adult education classes, no one testified that he would be willing to stay on the job for half the pay he could get somewhere else.

No one seemed to feel disloyal for doing this. In fact, people usually felt they would be disloyal to their families and themselves if they stayed on the job for so much less salary.

Yet, many of these same people were unwitting victims of the PHONY-LOYALTY GAME!

THE PHONY-LOYALTY DECLARATION:
"I pose as a good, honest and loyal employee in order to ingratiate myself with my employer and to insure my supply of security and other "goodies," which I am dependent upon him to supply."

AND NOW, LET'S TURN THE SITUATION AROUND.

Suppose someone approached your boss with an attractive deal. This person is able to do your job, easily, as well as you are doing it.

Imagine this individual offering to take over your job for *half-pay* – for exactly one-half of your salary.

How would you react if your boss called you in his office and said: "I regret this, especially after you have given six years of service to our company, but someone who can do your job equally well has offered to take it for one-half your salary.

"For the good of the company, I have accepted his offer. I have decided to terminate you. Sorry."

No doubt you would feel this was a gross injustice, or at least a ruthless act.

But – is there really a difference? Is there a difference between the principle of you leaving for double-salary and the boss replacing you for half-pay?

The point is clear: You do *not* work for your company out of *loyalty,* nor does your company employ you for sentimental reasons.

A winner recognizes this; Gary Goodman does not. A winner rejects the "Phony-Loyalty" game, and replaces it with the RULE OF RATIONAL SELF-INTEREST.

A good business must be run by certain rules of logic. A good business must make a profit to be secure as a sovereign entity. Businessmen recognize this fact. They are, for the most part, adept at putting profit before other considerations.

Some businessmen do much, very much that is brutal and ruthless in the name of "good business" and "for the good of the company." Whether or not this *should* be the case is not the issue; the fact is that *profit pragmatism* to the point of *actual ruthlessness* is a way of life in many businesses.

I have seen this "pragmatism" in operation many times. In the highest councils of businesses, too often an employee of many years' service is laid-off in the twinkling of an eye, or an executive under tremendous emotional strain is systematically isolated and destroyed without a second thought.

There is a valid reason for these surgically cold actions. A business is almost like a living entity, and profit is its lifeblood. Those who draw upon the company for subsistence *must preserve the company or their own lifeline will be severed.*

THE RULE OF RATIONAL-SELF INTEREST:

"Today I will be as hardnosed and pragmatic about my own welfare, maintenance, and future as the boss is about the maintenance, welfare, and future of his company. I will recall that I work for my boss only because, at the present time, it is in my own best interest to do so, and he employs me only because, at the present time, it is in his own best interest to do so."

The boss, especially, must fight and sweat and give his all to preserve and nurture his company; it is the source of not just material supply, but of all the ego and status rewards.

The more immature and weak the company, the more ruthless and violent it tends to be in its self-serving behavior.

RATIONAL SELF-INTEREST: A NEW AND TOUGHER WAY OF LIFE

In order to achieve a dynamic position as an employee of any company, you must learn to run your own career with the same pragmatic self-interest a good boss uses to run his business.

This requires some wise planning.

There follows a three-step planning approach that takes approximately an hour to execute. IT IS AN HOUR GUARANTEED TO CHANGE YOUR LIFE FOR THE BETTER.

STEP 1: WRITE DOWN, IN A FEW SENTENCES, YOUR OWN PHILOSOPHY OF THE "BUSINESS" OF YOUR LIFE.

Each enlightened business makes such a position statement, beginning with a clear, concise statement of its *reason for being,* to details of *what it plans to do in exchange for profit.*

When a consultant works with a business, it is common for him to request this simple philosophy statement (in written form of course).

Sometimes it takes weeks for various executives to agree on such a significant statement. Sometimes it is debated interminably.

Sooner or later a company must define its purpose (or admit that it simply has no definable purpose!).

THINK OF YOURSELF AND YOUR LIFE AS A BUSINESS ENTERPRISE

What *need* do you plan to *fill* as an individual, and how are you going to fill this need in exchange for personal reward? This personal reward may be material, social, spiritual or whatever you *really* desire it to be.

A good philosophy statement might modify the goals you have already written down. If it does not, you have selected your own goals accurately. *If it does conflict* with any goals you already have, *re-examine them.*

This statement is your WHY to live. A *will* to live is far less important than a WHY to live.

Viktor Frankle was a psychiatrist who was placed in a Nazi death camp during World War II. He lost family, home, career, and all his possessions.

Frankle lived with degrading torture, and constant threat of death. And yet he lived, and lived nobly. He secretly worked on a treatise, scribbling notes on scraps of paper. Later this work would become the basis of his Logotherapy theories.

Frankle explained that he survived because he had a WHY to live, he created a reason for continuing his life. He saw men and women around him languish and lose heart, their WHY to live, and eventually their will to live.

ATTITUDE — THE MAGIC WORD

Has any of us faced a situation as desolate as Frankle faced? Yet how many of us claim we are prevented from doing something worthwhile because of "circumstances!" It was *attitude* that saved Viktor Frankle.

Ponder carefully, and then write down (secretly) your own brief WHY to live statement, not to be "cast in stone" but rather to be something you modify as often as you feel appropriate. Get some writing materials and commit yourself right now.

This will not take you a very long time. Get something down now, don't try to be profound. Then you are ready for your second step.

STEP 2: WRITE OUT A 1-YEAR PLAN. (Even if your boss never wrote his business *philosophy* down, it is probable that he has some kind of an annual plan!)

Again, keep it simple. You have your goals; this is a 1-year time table.

STEP 3: A 5-YEAR PLAN. This can also be simple, but you must write down *where you want to be in 5 years.*

That is it. It works. (Each suggestion in this book is here because I know it works.) I NEVER COULD HAVE FINISHED THIS BOOK IF I HAD NOT WRITTEN DOWN PLANS. PRIOR TO DOING THAT I FLOUNDERED YEAR AFTER YEAR WITHOUT A SCHEDULE. WRITING MY OBJECTIVE DOWN AND SETTING A DATE FOR ITS ACCOMPLISHMENT HELPED MAKE IT HAPPEN.

My personal philosophy statement, one-year plan and five-year plan are written on two ordinary spiral notebook pages. I wrote them out in about an hour. Obviously, they are not detailed and tedious.

A good business *makes* things happen. A poor one *reacts* to what happens (I call this the "crisis of the week" syndrome). Likewise, a good life requires planning.

Without wise planning we go through life reacting to minor emergencies (usually one or more a day!).

• WITHOUT A GOAL, WE DRIFT.
• WITHOUT A COMPASS, WE ARE DIVERTED.
• WITHOUT A PLAN, WE NEVER KNOW WHETHER WE ARE GETTING ANYWHERE.

TODAY, MAKE A MEANINGFUL COMMITMENT . . . WRITE DOWN A PHILOSOPHY, A 1-YEAR AND 5-YEAR PLAN.

TODAY YOU BEGIN: • **THE NEXT-STEP STRATEGY**
                    • **THE MAIN-ISSUE MAXIM**
                    • **THE RULE OF RATIONAL SELF-INTEREST**

These are your *goal,* your *compass,* and your *timetable.*

Yet, you could still fall into a common trap. You could become a victim of the INITIATIVE-CRUSHING LOSER'S GAME, the terrible COMPETITIVE-ROBOT TREADMILL.

It is here, at this very point, that many worthy people fail.

POINTS TO REMEMBER:

THE NEXT-STEP STRATEGY
gives you a
GOAL...

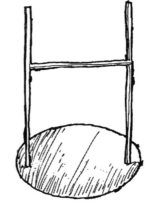

THE MAIN-ISSUE MAXIM
gives you a
COMPASS...

THE RULE OF RATIONAL SELF-INTEREST gives you a
TIMETABLE!

REFERENCES:

Joseph Sugarman: <u>SUCCESS FORCES</u>, Contemporary Books, Inc., Chicago, 1980

David Seaburg: <u>THE ART OF SELFISHNESS</u>, Cornerstone Library, New York, 1973

James K. VanFleet: <u>POWER WITH PEOPLE</u>, Parker Publishing Co., West Nyack, N.Y., 1970

George A. Stiener: <u>STRATEGIC PLANNING: WHAT EVERY MANAGER MUST KNOW</u>, Macmillan Company, New York, 1978

Viktor Frankle: <u>MAN'S SEARCH FOR MEANING</u>, Washington Square Press, New York, 1963

Dr. Fitzhugh Dodson with Paula Reuben: <u>THE YOU THAT COULD BE</u>, Follett Publishing Co., Chicago, 1976

Herbert A. Otto: <u>GUIDE TO DEVELOPING YOUR POTENTIAL</u>, Charles Scribner's Sons, New York, 1967

"I THINK I *HAVE* DONE SOMETHING GREAT," SAID JIM

ALMOST 15 years ago, I was enjoying a beer with a fellow I had known for several years. Jim was a remarkable guy. For eleven years he had been an employee of IBM. He was a predictable individual until he did an astonishing thing.

During the eleven years Jim was with IBM, he told everyone who knew him that he wanted to be a commercial artist. He studied hard at night. He took many courses in advertising and in art.

But Jim couldn't get a job as an artist. In the opinion of most employers he was too old at 31 to begin a new career. He had a family, and his income was too large to replace with a beginning artist's salary.

No one who knew Jim really believed he would ever make the move to commercial art. He was a nice guy, but he seemed security-motivated. An art career was becoming more and more risky to embark upon, as time went on.

Then Jim got an offer. For about half his current pay and no benefits, he could begin a job in a high-pressure art studio. The studio would guarantee him only two month's work. At that point, he was to be on his own.

It was a long shot. But even two months of experience would break the biggest barrier Jim had faced over and over: a lack of professional on-the-job experience. On the other hand, Jim would be sacrificing an eleven-year career with lots of security and a good future. No one who knew Jim would have predicted that he would make the move.

Jim surprised us all; he went for it. He quit his job at IBM, and began working at the agency. I thought he had flipped; I couldn't help feeling sorry for him.

Jim was in for some really rough times. His agency job was over in two months. He was laid off. Jim managed to hang on by getting a temporary job in a department store – strictly for the Christmas season overflow.

Two years later Jim headed the layout department of the store, and within three years he had moved to another company as an executive art director.

On this particular day, Jim and I were enjoying the atmosphere of the tavern, warm and cheerful in contrast to the Maryland winter day outside.

Someone played a record of Van Cliburn on the juke box. The great classical pianist had just made a trip to Russia, and had returned to unprecedented public acclaim.

"Gosh, he's great," said Jim.

"Yeah," I replied. "Just think what it would be like to have done something great in your life like Van Cliburn! Just one little taste of greatness! I wonder what it would feel like?"

Jim sat silently in thought. Then he said something that startled me.

"I think I HAVE done something great," he said.

"Come on, Jim! I mean really great! What have you done REALLY great?"

"I'll tell you. I quit my job at IBM, and I became an artist. After two weeks the people who hired me told me I wouldn't make it, and that I should go back to IBM. I told them that we had made a deal for two months, and I was staying.

"The only thing that sustained me was that on those long drives back and forth to work I kept saying to myself: 'YOU ARE AN ARTIST JIM! AT LAST, YOU ARE AN ARTIST!'"

"Everyone, including my wife, figured me for finished. But I hung in and made it. That, my friend, was great."

I couldn't believe my ears. "Jim, how can you compare that with something as monumental as Van Cliburn's talent?"

"I don't compare it. What I did was great *relative to my own potential.* I surpassed my own limitations; I achieved personal greatness. Deep down, I absolutely KNOW this is true.

"In fact, my achievement may have been greater, on that basis, than Van Cliburn's various accomplishments. But, it doesn't matter. I compare my achievements only to my potentials, not to his."

"Jim," I said, "with that criteria, anyone could be considered great."

"That's right. If an individual succeeds in transcending his limitations, he IS great. But, how many people actually do this? Most people live and die well within their comfort zone."

· · · · · ·

I thought about that conversation many times over the years. I never forgot it.

I now believe that Jim was right; greatness is relative. Achievement should be measured relative to estimated potential, not on some outside standard.

Jim had hit upon the RELATIVE-GREATNESS TECHNIQUE. He had learned to discard the destructive, miserable method of measuring success that most of us use: competing with something outside of ourselves.

Jim had escaped the most common of all employee traps, THE COMPETITIVE-ROBOT TREADMILL.

12

How To Get Off The "COMPETITIVE-ROBOT TREADMILL..."

...and Enjoy the Exhilarating Adventure of "Relative Greatness"

WE HAVE been programmed to believe that we must validate our worth by earning tangible *symbols* of accomplishment. These symbols are money, the things that money will buy, and evidence of recognition and prestige.

Each of these tangible symbols of accomplishment is earned by meeting some standard *outside of ourselves;* a standard imposed upon us by other minds.

Because we are programmed to meekly accept the yardstick of another "head," we place that opinion of our worth above our own. In other words, we become *dependent* upon that outside measurement.

This programmed reaction puts most of us on a "COMPETITIVE-ROBOT TREADMILL." Without thought, we automatically react to stimuli *outside of ourselves.*

We become afraid to try to get off of this treadmill. If we stop – even for a few minutes – someone will pass us by.

The Competitive-Robot Treadmill is a game of human robots, and can be stated as follows:

THE COMPETITIVE-ROBOT TREADMILL DECLARATION: "I validate or invalidate my own worth and progress by comparing how much money I make, how many status symbols I own, and how much recognition I have achieved with those same factors possessed by someone else."

This is a *dependency* game, a game of losers.

The vast majority of human beings in the world use precisely this system to measure their progress. People endure great agony in the pursuit of acquiring status symbols greater than those of their peers.

Somewhat more sophisticated individuals might say: "So what? This is the way we keep score, with money and things."

WHAT *IS* WRONG WITH MONEY?

Nothing is wrong with money. If accumulating money is a game, and you keep score with it, fine.

Yet, money is an inappropriate measurement of human worth. In the immature world of grown-up "children" we live in, criminals can acquire large sums of money; unscrupulous con men of all kinds can manipulate others and make a fortune; even professional degenerates are paid handsome sums of money to write about and to demonstrate debauchery. Virtually any individual who can entertain, from show business people to athletes, is paid incredible amounts of money to divert people from their humdrum lives.

A fortunate individual who is in the right place at the right time, can happen into vast amounts of money, yet a dedicated hard-working person can strive all his life and accumulate very little.

There are two basic ways of accumulating wealth: by being lucky and by planning wisely. The wise man maneuvers himself into the channels where wealth flows; the lucky man "falls into it." Yet the end result is the same – each man is wealthy.

Money is an appropriate measurement of one thing: How good or lucky you are at accumulating wealth.

Money does not make a man cultured, wise or talented. Money can give a degree of power, but power is hardly a measure of human worth.

Otherwise happy and balanced people can be reduced to a quivering, despairing, impotent rage by discovering that they make less money than someone else.

We are programmed to compete. What we need is a yardstick that is not dependent upon the opinion of those outside of ourselves. We need a means to validate our worth without becoming addicted to outside symbols and approval.

A NEW YARDSTICK BRINGS FREEDOM

Earlier we discussed the "inner core" of reality that Adler espoused. I would be remiss, and less than honest, if I failed to elaborate on this *most important* of all factors to your development and happiness.

Many people read books and try to learn things, to acquire more and more information about life. The idea seems to be that once we acquire enough knowledge, we will be better off and be able to master life. It is as though we believed that somewhere, buried in some paragraph, or about to be spoken by some great guru, is the "magic phrase" – the words that will turn our lives around.

We already have all the data we need. What we need is not more knowledge, but more *Being*. We need the "Inner Connection."

With the Inner Connection all the data we have falls into place. Additional data embellishes the perfectly contoured whole.

Without the Inner Connection all the data in the world will not help us. There are no "Magic Words."

Call this Inner Connection what you like. Call it your "higher inner self," call it God, or "The Force" – whatever term you select. From this inner core comes the infallible signals that help modulate your development to meet the challenges of an ever-unfolding, ever-new reality.

Virtually all the self-actualizing people studied by Abraham Maslow were aware of this personal, dynamic inner-reservoir of psychic being. Some of these people were professed atheists; others had deep religious convictions of nearly every type. The Inner Connection is independent of any formal religious persuasion.

The inner core of reality within us is the basis for the Relative-Greatness Technique. This system is totally independent of outside influences; it is an infallible gauge of progress.

When we have the initiative, when we are moving, we feel good. When we are asleep and dependent, we begin to feel inadequate, desolate, and discouraged.

We seem to sense that the process of motion toward our potential development is in tune with the universe; it is a natural high – a buoyant, positive state.

As Maslow discovered, self-actualizing people possess this kind of inner-life, not religious in the traditional sense, yet nonetheless a personal and real awareness of purpose and meaning.

When we have this Inner Connection we utilize more and more of our potentials; lacking this, we lose even those potentials we have. Without this Inner Connection lasting progress is not feasible.

HOW TO ACHIEVE THE INNER CONNECTION

The Inner Connection is simply a *receptive* state. It should be assumed as often as practical. It may last a few seconds, or several minutes.

It is not a means of escaping from life, but rather a means of revitalizing and co-ordinating our energies for the demanding struggle of life.

The less we feel like making the connection at a given time, the more we really need it.

There are many good techniques of meditation, of making the Inner Connection. The ones that are of low cost, or virtually free, seem as good as those that are expensive and elaborate.

Virtually all techniques are based upon a receptive state, achieved by letting go physically and mentally. (In the back of this chapter are several suggested books on the subject.)

Some techniques go a step further: In your receptive state you are asked to picture yourself as *in possession* of your particular goal. SEE YOURSELF AS GREAT, AS GREAT IN THE REAL SENSE – SEE YOURSELF AS EXCEEDING YOUR LIMITATIONS.

Make this picture as clear and real as possible. Be conscious of a power and inner direction . . . and *listen.*

Creative ideas will begin coming to you after these sessions. Keep a small notebook to record them. If you fail to record these ideas *they will slip away forever.* In my opinion, these ideas are your inner core giving you direction.

Now, at last, we shall try to define the RELATIVE-GREATNESS TECHNIQUE. It is A METHOD OF SELF-SOVEREIGNTY BASED UPON YOUR PERSONAL INNER CONNECTION, A CONSCIOUSNESS OF THE INNER REALITY, OF YOUR POTEN-TIALS MOVING TOWARD OUTWARD MANIFESTATION.

SEE YOURSELF AS GREAT!

THE
RELATIVE-GREATNESS
TECHNIQUE:

"Today I will take a few minutes to periodically establish my inner connection. I will seek greatness, RELATIVE to my POTENTIAL capabilities today, by surpassing those arbitrary limits I have placed upon myself."

The Relative-Greatness technique is not a measurement in the tangible sense; it is simply the conviction of motion. It is an unshakable belief that the actualizing process is taking place. When we lack this conviction, it is likely that we are in a *dependent condition* of some kind.

The very day that you stop relying on something "out there" to measure your worth, you will be free of the robot-like treadmill of comparison and competition.

RELATIVE GREATNESS: A FEW MORE SUGGESTIONS

Forget, for the moment, your distant goals. Picture yourself as you are today, and isolate your favorite fault.

Everybody has one. It is the one thing we would never sacrifice, it is our characteristic flaw.

In some people it is an addiction to booze, or sex, or gambling – or less dramatic – procrastination, money, ego food, security.

This is the characteristic that everyone who knows you takes for granted about you. Rather than a flaw, it is really an area of non-development.

In Jim's case, it was an addiction to security, to depending upon his job at IBM. We all knew, as his friends, that Jim could never transcend this need.

When Jim did strike out on the risky path he selected, *in spite of his fear,* we were all dumbfounded. We were also uncomfortable. *We wanted Jim to stay his mediocre self.*

It is very difficult for us to accept that someone we know has broken the mold we believe they belong in. We do not like people to "escape out of their circles."

For example, when someone who has been overweight for years goes on a diet, we do not like it. (Especially if we have a weight problem also!) We are certain they won't make it. If they do, we just know they will get fat again. So we COUNTER-VALUE their efforts, we make light of them. This protects us from the embarrassment of being shown up.

We don't want a friend to start jogging, to quit smoking, or to go back to school to become a doctor. We postulate into existence other people's limitations, and we expect them to stay within those limits.

We also postulate into existence our own limitations. This is our "circle area." If you take a step outside the area of the circles it is scary, heady stuff. And it will disturb just about everyone you know.

People, in general, want you to stay mediocre.

People do not want you to get a great job, a new car, or to get your picture in the paper. People do not want you to expose their mediocrity by your achievements.

When you transcend your limitations, your own comfort zone, you demonstrate Relative-Greatness. You must be prepared to possibly sacrifice the approval of others.

The sacrifice is well worth it.

IMAGINE YOURSELF GOING THROUGH A SINGLE DAY TRANSCENDING YOUR FAVORITE FAULT, FILLED WITH CONFIDENCE AND LOVE, AS THOUGH GOING TO SOME PRE-ARRANGED SUCCESS, TOWARD A LIFE OF BEAUTY AND SER-VICE, AS THOUGH YOUR WORTH IS VALIDATED NOW, IN SPITE OF THE CIRCUMSTANCES AND PEOPLE THAT NOW SURROUND YOU.

Imagine facing the very same problems that you face today as a new person, with a new, positive mental attitude. Imagine these problems melting away before the fire of this new greater you! Imagine mastering and USING your mind instead of being tortured by it; imagine tapping the reservoir of your potentials.

The RELATIVE-GREATNESS TECHNIQUE can be stated simply as the process of living up to the highest and best standards that you believe you are capable of reaching, and then *transcending* them.

This image, this standard, is the only gauge that you can depend upon, it puts no head above your own, and requires no other opinion but your own to certify your worth and progress.

This technique is predicated upon the ability of individ-uals to see themselves as more than they presently are. This is the prerequisite to beginning the self-actualizing process: You must believe that there really is a potential "higher you" to actualize. From the conviction that you *can* do, comes the *will* to do.

You have within you the WILL to handle all of your problems of today with grace and greatness. Virtually all true human failure is a crisis of will. First belief fails, and then will dissolves.

FREEDOM AND SELF-RELIANCE

The Relative-Greatness Technique frees you from the Competitive-Robot Treadmill, and the great difference between these two methods is important. We should review them:

THE COMPETITIVE-ROBOT TREADMILL is a system of competing with your peers for money, honors, status symbols, and so on. It puts some head higher than your own; it establishes something outside of you as a standard for performance.

The COMPETITIVE-ROBOT TREADMILL is a dependence system. You become dependent upon outside measurement, and addicted to those material symbols that seem to validate your success.

The RELATIVE-GREATNESS TECHNIQUE is an independent, self-contained method, and requires only your personal initiative and will to validate your success.

THE DEPENDENCY PATTERN

Now you can see a pattern developing in all the games that losers play. All 4 games we studied are *dependency games.*

QUICKLY TO REVIEW:

• **THE DRIFT-DELUSION:** waiting for something outside of yourself to give you direction.

• **THE MESSIANIC MISCONCEPTION:** being diverted by alluring "side shows" outside of your original, self-perceived goal, the "main event"...depending on something "out there" to fight and thus validate your own worth.

• **THE PHONY-LOYALTY GAME:** attempting to ingratiate yourself to outside forces in order to get the "goodies" of life.

• **THE COMPETITIVE-ROBOT TREADMILL:** requiring an outside standard of measurement to validate your worth and progress.

The alternative games of winners are games of self-reliance and initiative: THE NEXT-STEP STRATEGY, THE MAIN-ISSUE MAXIM, THE RULE OF RATIONAL SELF-INTEREST, AND THE RELATIVE-GREATNESS TECHNIQUE.

With this in mind, let's examine the final game of losers, the most deadly of all human traps. It is the most popular loser game ever created, the game of the perpetual victim, the DIVINE MISERY of MARTYRDOM.

POINTS TO REMEMBER:

THE WORLD WANTS YOU TO STAY MEDIOCRE...

THE BEST YOU CAN BE IS... MEDIOCRE!

OH, YEAH?

RELATIVE GREATNESS....
is the process of living up to the highest and best that is in us each day by
SURPASSING THE ARBITRARY SELF-LIMITS WE AND OTHER PEOPLE HAVE POSTULATED AS "FACT"

REFERENCES:

Willard & Marguerite Beecher: BEYOND SUCCESS AND FAILURE: WAYS TO SELF-RE-LIANCE AND MATURITY, Pocket Books, New York, 1975

Jose Silva and Philip Miele: THE SILVA-MIND CONTROL METHOD, Simon and Schuster, New York, 1977

Maxwell Maltz: PSYCO-CYBERNETICS, Simon and Schuster, New York, 1960

Donald L. Wilson, M.D.: TOTAL MIND POWER, Berkley Publishing Company, New York, 1978

H. Benson: THE RELAXATION RESPONSE, William Morrow and Company, Inc., New York, 1975

Barbara Brown: NEW MIND, NEW BODY, BIOFEEDBACK: NEW DIRECTIONS FOR THE MIND, Bantam Books, New York, 1975

Sheila Ostrander and Lynn Schroeder with Nancy Ostrander: SUPER LEARNING, Delacorte Press, New York, 1979

Abraham Maslow: RELIGIOUS VALUES AND PEAK EXPERIENCES, Penguin Books, New York, 1976

Abraham Maslow: TOWARD A PSYCHOLOGY OF BEING, D. Van Nostrand Company, New York, 1968

William Glasser, M.D.: POSITIVE ADDICTION, Harper and Row, New York, 1976

Yogi Ramacharaka: RAJA YOGA OR MENTAL DEVELOPMENT, The Yogi Publishing Society, Chicago, 1934

P. D. Ouspensky: THE PSYCHOLOGY OF MAN'S POSSIBLE EVOLUTION, Vintage Books, New York, 1974

Ken Keyes, Jr.: THE HANDBOOK TO HIGHER CONSCIOUSNESS, Living Love Center, Berkeley, California, 1972

A TEAR TRICKLED DOWN LOUIS' CHEEK

L OUIS THE XIV was one of most blatant, arrogant, and insensitive monarchs of all time. Spoiled and vain, Louis seemed totally indifferent to the poverty of the French people. He squandered money for his own opulent tastes, and waged costly wars for sport.

Louis lived in unparalleled luxury. The royal family often enjoyed an incredibly expensive breakfast in the open courtyard of the palace, while hungry peasants watched through the gate. Louis thought they were admiring him.

Louis was insulated from reality. He was praised from all sides by the sycophants of the French court. Louis fancied himself a great military leader and an ingenious general. He took credit for all the victories his troops and officers achieved.

When fortune turned against Louis, he began to lose battle after battle. He could not cope.

One day a messenger brought news of a particularly catastrophic defeat. The poor man was terrified as he watched the face of Louis darken in fury.

A tear trickled down the powdered cheek of Louis. The dumbfounded messenger had no idea what the eccentric monarch would do.

Louis collapsed harmlessly in a royal chair.

"God has forgotten all I have done for him," Louis said.

13

A Sure Cure For The "DIVINE MISERY OF MARTYRDOM"

...The "Resolution of Responsibility"

NEARLY EVERY human being loves to be a martyr. Not only the simple, everyday folks, but also the famous and the infamous as well.

Gary Goodman and Fred Fridgide are perfect martyr candidates, of course. Harry Haight and even Mike Mature can be pushed to the breaking point and yield to the great temptation for self-pity.

Even the toughest people, when defeated and forced to the brink of disaster, find great solace in the wine of self-compassion – and a single sip can numb the mind for days.

Louis the XIV could not face defeat; he blamed God for his misfortune. In the '30's a bloodthirsty killer named 2-gun Crowley murdered several innocent people in cold blood, including a policeman whom Crowley shot without provocation or warning.

Did Crowley regret his deeds when he faced execution? Not at all. He said: "This is what I get for trying to defend myself." Crowley saw *himself* as the wronged party – the *victim!*

Adolf Hitler went down to defeat, amid the burning ruins of Berlin, blaming the Jews for starting the War, the German people for not being worthy of him, and the general staff for not executing his orders! This macabre butcher saw *himself* as the *victim* of others!

Some people are absolutely brilliant at living in perpetual martyrdom and victimhood. No matter what the situation, it is soon twisted until it can be made to justify their own chronic indignant rage or hurt feelings.

Few people uncompromisingly accept the responsibility for themselves and their lives. Thus was created the most popular loser's game in the world: THE DIVINE MISERY OF MARTYRDOM. The Creed of the perpetual martyr follows.

THE DIVINE MISERY OF MARTYRDOM DECLARATION :
"I am not a free human being; I am a victim. I live in the environment I do, I am where I am in life, I associate with the people I do, have the attitudes I do, because of circumstances beyond my control. I am dependent upon the good will of others (which is not dependable!) as well as pure luck to supply the 'goodies' in life I want and need."

Most people would not make this declaration out loud, of course, but *they ACT as though this philosophy ruled their lives.*

The unconscious dependence upon others is a subtle, destructive factor. The Divine Misery of Martyrdom postulates the responsibility of other people for your own problems, and your unhappiness.

This martyrdom posture implies that *you are helpless* to create and control your own environment, and that you are a noble victim of evil, selfish people.

Responsibility, and thus authority over your life, are handed over to others by default, in the hope that they will be nice enough to feel sorry for you or be intimidated by your outrage and do what you want them to do.

This avoidance of personal responsibility is perhaps the most common syndrome of losers.

To validate that statement, listen to the conversations around you. Listen to the complaints, the groans at the lunch counters, in the break-rooms, in the subways. Note the negative helplessness of most people as they bristle with rage and indignation about the injustice of something, or someone.

Passive people, like Fred Fridgide, play the Game of The Divine Misery of Martyrdom with superb skill. They are chronic, ingrained martyrs.

Most other people who tend to believe themselves, at times, to be victims of injustice are *reactive* martyrs. They have temporarily lost their courage and confidence. (Note, please, that I said LOST their courage and confidence. No one can take their courage away from them – they must *lose* it on their own.)

When frustration leverages a person into a secondary behavior, they usually assume a Hostile/Timid pattern. In this mode, martyrdom comes easy.

Some people were beaten down and fell into the martyrdom complex early; some take it up later in life. One thing is sure, if it is indulged in too long, it becomes a way of life.

The allure of martyrdom is hard to resist; being a victim has several distinct advantages.

- **BEING A VICTIM:**
  - ASSURES YOU OF BEING *INNOCENT,* ABSOLVES YOU FROM THE RESPONSIBILITY FOR YOUR LIFE.
  - AFFORDS YOU THE DELICIOUS RIGHT TO COMPLAIN, GRIPE AND RAIL AT CIRCUMSTANCES AND PEOPLE.
  - BESTOWS THE PRIVILEGE OF UNBOUNDED SELF-PITY.
  - SOLVES FOREVER ANY FURTHER CONJECTURE ABOUT RIGHT AND WRONG: YOU ARE AN INNOCENT VICTIM, AND THUS YOU ARE RIGHT – THE EVIL FORCES THAT THWART YOU ARE, OF COURSE, WRONG.

Notwithstanding the advantages of the Divine Misery of Martyrdom, there are also disadvantages. In fact, no single game is more certain to insure a life of mediocrity.

Victims of martyrdom live a joyless life, because the indulgence of this "noble" state deprives them of the eternal *now*.

Resentment, anger, regret, fear, guilt, – all these things pull you out of the present and into the regretful past, or into the threatening future.

Chewing the cud of regret, of injustice, and of vanished joys steals the one thing that *is* real, the here and now.

What is really needed is freedom from the tyranny of victimhood and self-pity. What is needed is the personal assumption of self-sovereignty and self-mastery.

Giving up your rights to martyrdom will be difficult. Yet in virtually every great life there must come that supreme moment – the assumption of responsibility. It may come early, or it may come late in life, but come it must. In order to be free, you must claim your birthright by force.

THE RESOLUTION OF RESPONSIBILITY

The alternative to martyrdom is the irrevocable decision to accept self-responsibility and self-initiative. This decision rejects forever your dependence upon the good will of others for the "goodies" of life, including approval, love, esteem, and power.

The RESOLUTION OF RESPONSIBILITY is a declaration of freedom from the self-pitying narcotic of martyrdom.

THE RESOLUTION OF RESPONSIBILITY:

"I am a free human being, I am not a victim. I live in the environment I do, I am where I am in life, I associate with the people I do, have the attitudes I do, because of circumstances I have created or permitted to exist. I am capable of achieving whatever I can intelligently determine to achieve, and I am responsible for my situation. No one can rescue me, but mighty forces will come to my aid when I begin to make growth decisions and *complete them through positive ACTION.*"

This resolution is the last of our winning games; it is the *final critical decision,* the ultimate growth choice for the self-actualizing human being.

Much of the agony of life is not predicated upon unfavorable circumstances, but rather upon the dependent attitudes of people toward those circumstances.

Generally, no matter what the situation, if one is resolute enough there is virtually always a *solution of attitude* – not to endure situations, but to solve or transcend them utterly.

It was *attitude* that saved Viktor Frankle from death in a Nazi concentration camp. It was attitude that made Helen Keller's life a beacon unto the world, rather than a dark, silent, tragic prison.

It is attitude that will turn your own world around. The assumption of personal responsibility is obviously a whole new way of life.

There is a magic moment in every successful psychotherapy case, a moment when the patient assumes responsibility for himself. It may take some time, but this precious moment of clarity seems to be a supreme human insight.

No one has real power over you – unless you postulate such a situation into reality. Selfish people are not to blame for your failures, but they are ever-ready to exploit your dependency.

At the beginning of this book, I said that management might very well be to blame for the fact that you will only develop 1/10 of your potential. If this book has done its job, management no longer has the power to totally frustrate your development.

You can see now, I hope, that only dependent, immature people can long be exploited by immature management. Let's take a final look at the immature loser and his games. He is asleep, addicted to security, approval, ego or power needs, and so he is exploitable. The immature employee plays the game within the "circles." This keeps him fairly safe, but forever a loser.

The mature employee is far more free. He is unfolding and creative. In place of dependency games, he plays the exhilarating winner's games.

You must choose the games you play, even if you do so by default.

THE LOSER'S MEDIOCRITY MANIFESTO

1. THE DRIFT-DELUSION DECLARATION:

"I am keeping my talent, my real enthusiasm, and my sincere commitment on hold until I discover what it is that I really want to do, or until the heavens open up and God speaks to direct me to some noble endeavor of supreme magnitude."

2. THE MESSIANIC MISCONCEPTION DECLARATION:

"I can pursue my main goal and still have time and energy to compete with others, and to correct the methods and attitudes of the individuals and organizations with which I must deal."

3. THE PHONY-LOYALTY DECLARATION:

"I pose as a good, honest, and loyal employee in order to ingratiate myself with my employer and to insure my supply of security and other "goodies" which I am dependent upon him to supply."

4. THE COMPETITIVE-ROBOT TREADMILL DECLARATION:

"I validate or invalidate my own worth and progress by comparing how much money I make, how many status symbols I own, and how much recognition I have achieved with those same factors possessed by someone else."

5. THE DIVINE MISERY OF MARTYRDOM DECLARATION:

"I am not a free human being, I am a victim. I live in the environment I do, I am where I am in life, I associate with the people I do, have the attitudes I do because of circumstances beyond my control. I am dependent upon the good will of others (which is not dependable!) as well as pure luck to supply the "goodies" in life I want and need."

239

THE WINNER'S MANIFESTO

THE MASTER STRATEGY OF ACTION AND MOVEMENT

1. THE NEXT-STEP STRATEGY:

"Today I will exert the very best there is in me
to move toward the accomplishment of my own
personal NEXT-STEP. This is the constructive step
I have known for a long time I should take, but I
continue to procrastinate and fail to act. Today
I will begin movement toward that step so that the
NEXT Next-Step can appear."

2. THE MAIN-ISSUE MAXIM:

"Today I will exert all my effort to focus upon the
MAIN ISSUE of my life, my NEXT-STEP, and will
shun all ego food and ignore all unrelated issues.
I will use existing systems, people and institutions
to accomplish my objectives."*

*Unless, of course, your specific *single* major objective is to change one of those factors.

3. THE RULE OF RATIONAL SELF-INTEREST:

"Today I will be as hardnosed and pragmatic about
my own welfare, maintenance, and future, as the
boss is about the maintenance, welfare, and future
of his company. I will recall that I work for my
boss only because, at the present time, it is in my
own best interest to do so, and he employs me only
because, at the present time, it is in his own best
interest to do so."

5. THE RESOLUTION OF RESPONSIBILITY:

"I am a free human being, I am not a victim. I live in the environment I do, I am where I am in life, I associate with the people I do, have the attitudes I do, because of circumstances I have created or permitted to exist. I am capable of achieving whatever I can intelligently determine to achieve, and I am responsible for my situation. No one can rescue me, but mighty forces will come to my aid when I begin to make growth decisions and *complete them through positive ACTION."*

4. THE RELATIVE-GREATNESS TECHNIQUE:

"Today I will take a few minutes to periodically establish my inner connection. I will seek greatness, RELATIVE to my POTENTIAL capabilities today, by surpassing those arbitrary limits I have placed upon myself."

HOW TO REPROGRAM YOUR MIND TO WIN

The two philosophies on the preceding pages represent two widely different points of view. One is positive; one is negative.

The loser's manifesto is presented because most people ACT as though they believe what it says. The winner's manifesto is something people tend to pay lip service to, but few people ACT as though they really believe.

One method that is very successful in reconditioning a mind into positive thinking is the technique of affirmations. An affirmation is a repetitive suggestion that is repeated over and over again until it is believed. Obviously, a positive affirmation is intended to create a positive state of mind.

Personally, I have had very good success with this method. It is important to develop a statement that fits you, that is in your own words. Read it aloud at least once a day, possibly right after one of your "INNER CONNECTION" sessions. Another excellent time for affirmations is in the morning, as a sort of breakfast for the mind. A positive affirmation FOCUSES your mind upon success and positive thoughts, as opposed to the drift method which may, or may not, get your mind going in a positive channel.

An associate of mine has had absolutely incredible success with the affirmation method. He periodically TAPES his on a cassette, and then LISTENS to it every day, at least once.

By using this tape method, and jogging in place each day while he listened to his affirmation, the man went from being $30,000 in debt and bankruptcy to an annual income approaching a MILLION DOLLARS NET! He gives credit to the system, and it is hard to doubt him.

By the way, this individual also claims that good luck seemed to begin to happen to him when he began using the affirmation technique.

Try it yourself. The affirmation technique is used in nearly all forms of self-help and self-motivation progams. Use the winner's affirmations suggested or your own equivalent, and add some of your own goals and aspirations.

State your goals boldly and confidently. TAKE YOUR TIME. GIVE A DATE THAT YOU WILL ACHIEVE EACH GOAL. Don't *memorize* words, but keep ideas and pictures in mind and express them as you wish.

Affirmations seem to penetrate deep into the mind and tap some reservoir of strength. If this exercise of using affirmations is of help to you, investigate some of the current books being written on the subject.

Avoid at all costs the habit of some people who read all about success, and then fail to actually DO any of the techniques urged by author after author. They fail to write down goals, but they READ about writing down goals. They fail to use affirmations, but they READ about using affirmations. It is as though the process of reading and contemplating action becomes the whole activity. Soon reading crystallizes into a kind of fantasy game that never really is tested in the cold, rugged light of reality. Imagination becomes a substitute for action.

The five winner's games collectively comprise the MASTER STRATEGY. Each game plays a part in the incredible synergism of this Master Strategy. If you omit one component, you virtually negate the power of the whole system.

THE LOSER DEPENDENCY GAMES...
(The "Games Without End")

THE DRIFT-DELUSION...
Passively waits for outside
stimulus before acting

**THE MESSIANIC
MISCONCEPTION...**
Diverts the main thrust to "side-
show" activities, and fails to
focus upon the "main event"

THE PHONY-LOYALTY GAME...
Ingratiates self to boss and
others to acquire the "goodies"
to which individual is addicted

**THE COMPETITIVE-ROBOT
TREADMILL...** Competes
mindlessly with others and
seeks to validate worth by
comparing material gains and
status with those of others

**THE DIVINE MISERY OF
MARTYRDOM...** The victim
philosophy. Blames something
"out there" for failures
and unhappiness

THE GAMES OF FREEDOM
AND INDEPENDENCE...

THE NEXT-STEP STRATEGY...
An unfailing goal-setting
philosophy that will end
procrastination and
rationalization

THE MAIN-ISSUE MAXIM...
The "compass" that keeps you
resolutely focused upon
your goals

**THE RULE OF RATIONAL
SELF-INTEREST...** The
Timetable part of the
MASTER STRATEGY helps
you operate your life with the
same pragmatism your boss
applies to business

POINTS TO REMEMBER:

—EVEN IF YOU READ a thousand books and study hundreds of theories, you will never stimulate the dynamics you need for change until you ACT, until you take the NEXT STEP.

—NO MATTER HOW CLEVER you are, and aggressively you behave, you'll never achieve what you might achieve if you cannot focus upon the MAIN ISSUE of your life and use skillfully, and with surgical coldness, the existing systems, people and means available to achieve it.

—YOUR BOSS WILL ALWAYS be able to exploit and treat you like a pawn until you are able to be as pragmatic and hardnosed about your PERSONAL INTERESTS, your career, your welfare, maintenance and development, as he is about his business' maintenance, welfare, and development.

—THE COMPETITIVE-ROBOT TREADMILL will keep you fighting until you are burned out unless you develop the INNER CONNECTION, and learn to use the RELATIVE-GREATNESS TECHNIQUE.

—IF YOU DO NOT DECLARE the RESOLUTION OF RESPONSIBILITY for yourself and take your life in your own hands you may drift through this world as one of the noble, "honest" victims of unscrupulous people and unjust circumstances . . . a loser.

THE RESOLUTION OF RESPONSIBILITY . . . The supreme resolution that permits you to claim sovereignty over your life

THE RELATIVE-GREATNESS TECHNIQUE . . . A completely independent evaluation system that monitors your progress with unfailing accuracy

REFERENCES:

Robert S. DeRopp: <u>WARRIORS WAY</u>, Dell Publishing Co., New York, 1979

William Warren Barkley: <u>WERNER ERHARD, THE TRANSFORMATION OF A MAN: THE FOUNDING OF EST</u>, Charles N. Potter, New York, 1978

Ralph Waldo Emerson: <u>SELF RELIANCE</u>, Peter Pauper Press, Mount Vernon, New York, 1967

Roberto Assagioli, M.D.: <u>THE ACT OF WILL</u>, Penguin Books, New York, 1974

Willard and Marguerite Beecher: <u>BEYOND SUCCESS AND FAILURE, WAYS TO SELF-RELIANCE AND MATURITY</u>, Pocket Books, New York, 1975

Wayne Dyer: <u>YOUR ERRONEOUS ZONES</u>, Funk and Wagnalls, New York, 1976

Dr. Wayne Dyer: <u>THE SKY'S THE LIMIT</u>, Simon and Schuster, New York, 1980

Frank G. Goble: <u>THE THIRD FORCE, THE SCIENCE OF SELF-ACTUALIZATION</u>, Grossman Publishing, New York, 1970

DON'T YOU WANT TO DESTROY YOUR ENEMIES?" THE WOMAN ASKED.

THE MOST bloody war in American history, the most costly in human lives and suffering, was the Civil War. Hatred ran deeper than we can dream of today. So much destruction and bloodletting took place that it seemed the wounds would never heal.

Near the end of the war the Union closed a vise of steel upon the gallant South, and slashed mercilessly through the once beautiful land, laying it to waste.

Revenge was on the minds of the Northerners. They believed that the South should pay for the horrible ordeal that had torn the country asunder.

In this mood of vengeance only a few individuals held back the tides of unbridled hate.

Abraham Lincoln sat working at his desk one day, near the very end of the conflict. He was signing pardons for many of the Southern leaders, some of whom the radicals wanted summarily executed.

A secretary assisting Lincoln was astonished at the leniency of the great man. With strokes of his pen he was saving life after life. In fact, he saved lives belonging to men who would have relished the destruction of Abraham Lincoln.

Finally the secretary said in a distraught voice: "Mr. President, don't you want to *destroy* your enemies?"

Lincoln looked up with patient, kind eyes and replied: "Is that not what I do when I make them my friends?"

14

Before I Turn You Over To THE UNICORN

...a Few Final Suggestions

N O ONE has all the answers. In fact, few people have any of the answers.

In the pages of this book you may find, if not any answers, at least a few threads – threads that need to be followed and developed. There is more, very much more, to be learned.

We have skimmed over some profound questions – only able to touch the surface of some topics. Self-actualization is a subject as vast as human potential itself, and for you it will be a journey of supreme significance.

Continue to learn, and trust your own judgment. Consider a book like this as a kind of cafeteria, with ideas offered rather than food. Accept only those things which ring true. Pass by the other ideas, but don't reject them. The day may come when you will want to come back and pick up an idea you earlier passed by as inappropriate.

Involve yourself with mankind. Understanding (to a degree), the motivation of immature people will help you to endure them and even care for them. Thus you may learn to destroy your enemies in the only cosmically acceptable way, by making them your friends.

In the beginning of this book we made a statement that should be reconsidered in the light of what we've learned: As children we were loved, and everything seemed brighter and more beautiful. The process of maturity is the process of *learning to love,* of learning to *give back* love to the world, instead of seeking to *take* it.

It is a bit easier to accept people when you understand that virtually every ugly and annoying action by the human creature is simply an attempt to *take love,* long after the need to be loved should have been supplanted by the desire to *give love.*

Strive for balanced development. Obviously an individual cannot eat or drink like a madman and expect to live a graceful, poised life.

Nor can an individual go on to higher things when his intimate life is awry. If yours is distorted, correct it and then begin your quest.

In my judgment, there will come a day when the business community is dominated by the service motive, rather than the pure profit motive. Perhaps this seems like a Quixote-like vision now, but there are favorable signs of transition for those who would see them.

Until that distant day of enlightened self-interest by the business world, I leave you with one final concept. We have discussed it before, and it is, indeed, the theme of this book.

The wonderful musical play MAN OF LA MANCHA was based upon the story by Miguel de Cervantes: DON QUIXOTE. The tale is about an old, senile Don who wandered over the parched lands of Spain trying to rekindle the past glories of knighthood, chivalry and idealism. The poor, befuddled Don Quixote could not seem to comprehend that he was surrounded by selfishness and evil. He seemed to see but a fantasy of good.

Finally, the alarmed family of Don Quixote sent two friends to fetch him back home.

These two men, a doctor and a priest, beseeched the Don to return to his family. They warned him that he does not see reality as it is. The doctor tells him that he must come to terms with life "as it is."

Don Quixote made an amazing reply. He said that he had seen life as it is. He had seen the incredible cruelty, the agony, and the joy of human beings. Quixote said that he had been a soldier, and he told of holding his dying comrades in his arms. He noted that he had heard no great last words from these men, but only heard them murmur "Why?" in the final moments. Their confusion did not seem to be about why they were dying, but rather *why they had lived.* Finally, the Don asserts that perhaps the maddest thing in all the world was to see life *as it is,* rather than to see it *as it ought to be.*

Over many years I have seen business as it is. I have seen human potential lie fallow and watched incentive become blunted or crushed altogether by immature people with power. I have also seen a few human comets transcend these restrictions, and blaze gloriously in valiant pursuit of some worthy objective, some cause larger than themselves. I have often sat across a lunch table and observed the vacant eyes of the walking wounded, those who have somehow lost (or perhaps never found) a WHY to live. For those unfortunate people there seemed to be no joy, no hope, no dream, but rather only a puzzlement about why they were here at all.

The difference between the hollow-eyed losers and the brilliant achievers always seemed to stem from the achiever's conviction that there *is,* indeed, *meaning and purpose to life.* Once a human creature is really convinced that this is true, it seems he will walk through walls and swim oceans to *find* that meaning and purpose.

Surely, each of us needs this single starting point, this supreme *decision* that somewhere, submerged within the agony and pain of life, is a priceless treasure worth many times its enormous cost. Once we acknowledge that it is there, we shall surely find it. This remarkable treasure is our personal quest, our own "impossible dream." It is this unique personal obsession that will fill the sky with light, and bring meaning to lives too often brimming with things, but impoverished of values.

It is the birthright of each of us to be a visionary on some significant scale, and it is the visionaries who have been the salvation of humankind. It is the Frank Lloyd Wrights, the Walt Disneys, the Hellen Kellers, who have enriched this planet with their ability to live *as though seeing that which cannot be seen,* of being able to perceive life, not simply as it is, but also as it *ought to be.*

Go forth and make some monster company a bit more human. Create an enclave of compassion out of a single office, or a desk, or some modest area. Or, go out and build a company of your own – an enlightened, human company.

See life as it *ought to be,* and try to make your own part of it that way. Become one of the idealistic elite of this day, and this generation.

As we said at the beginning, the world desperately needs more energetic, compassionate, active people, more leaders who trust and believe in the noble potential of themselves and of other human beings. The world needs people who are willing to expend the effort and make the sacrifices necessary to regain the planet from the weaklings and grown up "children" who have too long saturated it with misery and exploitation.

Are you destined to be one of these new leaders?

If not you, then who?

POINTS TO REMEMBER:

EMMETT FOX BELIEVED that if you are resolute in your efforts at self development, one day a unicorn will be waiting for you outside your door.

The unicorn will be snorting and impatiently pawing the earth, and he will not wait long for you, nor will he take orders from you.

Leap upon his back, and he will carry you off to places that are beyond your wildest dreams and imaginings.
It's true, my friend.

Good Luck,

Larry Mullins

REFERENCES:

Arnold Michael: THE DISCIPLINE OF DELIGHT, Scrivener & Company, Los Angeles, 1970

Ken Keyes, Jr.: HANDBOOK TO HIGHER CONSCIOUSNESS, Living Love Center, Berkeley, California, 1972

Emmett Fox: AROUND THE YEAR, Harper & Bros., New York, 1952

Dale Wasserman, Joe Darion, Mitch Leigh: MAN OF LA MANCHA, A Random House Play, ©1966 Dale Wasserman

IMMATURE PEOPLE WITH POWER ... How to Handle Them
is based upon seminars developed over several years for schools, universities, and businesses. For additional information on a program tailored to your organizational needs, contact:

LARRY MULLINS
METAVALUES® PROGRAMS
904.794.9212

Employees, CEOs, middle managers, salespersons, hospitality professionals, and many others will all find common ground in *Immature People with Power ... How to Handle Them.*

We strongly urge you to introduce these concepts to your own circle of friends. Consider giving kindred spirits a copy of this book. If you have your own website or blog, consider sharing your experiences there.

Write a review of *Immature People with Power ... How to Handle Them* for your newspaper or post it on *www.amazon.com*. Ask your company, college, or association to invite Larry Mullins as a guest speaker. Visit our website *www.larrymullins.com* to watch our progress and learn more about our projects, activities and opportunities.

FREE BONUS
for Readers of Immature People with Power ... How to Handle Them

If you would like more information on the practical application of the concepts in this book to your business or profession, you can download several free illustrated articles from:

www.larrymullins.com/ipwp/

BUY A SHARE OF THE FUTURE IN YOUR COMMUNITY

These certificates make great holiday, graduation and birthday gifts that can be personalized with the recipient's name. The cost of one S.H.A.R.E. or one square foot is $54.17. The personalized certificate is suitable for framing and will state the number of shares purchased and the amount of each share, as well as the recipient's name. The home that you participate in "building" will last for many years and will continue to grow in value.

Here is a sample SHARE certificate:

THIS CERTIFIES THAT

YOUR NAME HERE

HAS INVESTED IN A HOME FOR A DESERVING FAMILY

1985-2005

TWENTY YEARS OF BUILDING FUTURES IN OUR
COMMUNITY ONE HOME AT A TIME

1200 SQUARE FOOT HOUSE @ $65,000 = $54.17 PER SQUARE FOOT
This certificate represents a tax deductible donation. It has no cash value.

YES, I WOULD LIKE TO HELP!

I support the work that Habitat for Humanity does and I want to be part of the excitement! As a donor, I will receive periodic updates on your construction activities but, more importantly, I know my gift will help a family in our community realize the dream of homeownership. I would like to SHARE in your efforts against substandard housing in my community! (Please print below)

PLEASE SEND ME _____ SHARES at $54.17 EACH = $ $_____

In Honor Of: _____

Occasion: (Circle One)   HOLIDAY   BIRTHDAY   ANNIVERSARY

      OTHER: _____

Address of Recipient: _____

Gift From: _____ *Donor Address:* _____

Donor Email: _____

I AM ENCLOSING A CHECK FOR $ $_____ PAYABLE TO HABITAT FOR HUMANITY OR PLEASE CHARGE MY VISA OR MASTERCARD *(CIRCLE ONE)*

Card Number _____ Expiration Date: _____

Name as it appears on Credit Card _____ Charge Amount $ _____

Signature _____

Billing Address _____

Telephone # Day _____ Eve _____

PLEASE NOTE: Your contribution is tax-deductible to the fullest extent allowed by law.
Habitat for Humanity • P.O. Box 1443 • Newport News, VA 23601 • 757-596-5553
www.HelpHabitatforHumanity.org